Better Homes and Gardens®

Hometown

FAVORITES

Delicious down-home recipes

Volume 7

Meredith Consumer Marketing
Des Moines, Iowa

Better Homes and Gardens®

Hometown Favorites

MEREDITH CONSUMER MARKETING
Vice President, Consumer Marketing: Janet Donnelly
Consumer Marketing Product Director: Heather Sorensen
Consumer Marketing Product Manager: Wendy Merical
Consumer Marketing Billing/Renewal Manager: Tami Beachem
Business Director: Ron Clingman
Senior Production Manager: Al Rodruck

WATERBURY PUBLICATIONS, INC.
Editorial Director: Lisa Kingsley
Associate Editor: Tricia Bergman
Creative Director: Ken Carlson
Associate Design Director: Doug Samuelson
Contributing Art Director: Mindy Samuelson
Contributing Writer: Lisa Kingsley
Contributing Copy Editors: Carrie Schmitz, Peg Smith
Contributing Indexer: Elizabeth T. Parson

BETTER HOMES AND GARDENS® MAGAZINE
Editor in Chief: Gayle Goodson Butler
Deputy Editor, Food and Entertaining: Nancy Wall Hopkins

MEREDITH NATIONAL MEDIA GROUP
President: Tom Harty

MEREDITH CORPORATION
Chairman and Chief Executive Officer: Stephen M. Lacy

In Memoriam: E.T. Meredith III (1933–2003)

Better Homes and Gardens® Test Kitchen

Our seal assures you that every recipe in *Hometown Favorites* has been tested in the Better Homes and Gardens® Test Kitchen. This means that each recipe is practical and reliable, and it meets our high standards of taste appeal. We guarantee your satisfaction with this book for as long as you own it.

All of us at Meredith Consumer Marketing are dedicated to providing you with information and ideas to enhance your home. We welcome your comments and suggestions. Write to us at: Meredith Consumer Marketing, 1716 Locust St., Des Moines, IA 50309-3023.

Pictured on front cover:
Chocolate Picnic Cake, page 162
Photography by Karla Conrad

Contents

CHAPTER 1

Appetizers

Get the party started—and keep it going—with these savory nibbles and refreshing drinks for both intimate gatherings and big celebrations.

9

19

27

Coffee-Marinated Beef Kabobs with Aïoli

This Americanized take on Indonesian satay features beef instead of chicken or pork—and rich, garlicky homemade mayo dipping sauce in place of peanut sauce.

PREP 40 minutes
CHILL 2 hours
SOAK 30 minutes
BROIL 4 minutes

12 servings	ingredients	24 servings
1 lb.	boneless beef sirloin steak, cut 1 inch thick	2 lb.
¼ cup	strong brewed coffee	½ cup
¼ cup	dry red wine	½ cup
¾ tsp.	coarsely ground pepper	1½ tsp.
½ tsp.	salt	1 tsp.
⅛ tsp.	cayenne pepper	¼ tsp.
5 cloves	garlic, minced	10 cloves
¼ cup	refrigerated or frozen egg product, thawed	½ cup
2 Tbsp.	fresh lemon juice	4 Tbsp.
¼ tsp.	salt	½ tsp.
¾ cup	olive oil	1½ cups

1. Cut steak across the grain into long, thin strips. Place strips in a sealable plastic bag; set bag in a shallow dish.

2. For marinade, stir together coffee, wine, black pepper, ½ teaspoon salt, and the cayenne pepper; pour over meat in bag. Seal bag. Chill for 2 to 4 hours, turning bag once or twice.

3. Drain meat strips, discarding marinade. Thread strips accordion-style onto twelve 6-inch skewers.* Place kabobs on the unheated rack of a broiler pan. Broil 3 to 4 inches from heat for 4 to 6 minutes or until desired doneness, turning once.

4. Meanwhile, for aïoli, in a blender or food processor combine garlic, egg product, lemon juice, and ¼ teaspoon salt. Cover and blend or process for 5 seconds or until smooth. With blender or food processor running, gradually add olive oil in a thin, steady stream, stopping machine as necessary to scrape sides.

5. To serve, arrange kabobs on a serving platter. Serve with aïoli.**

*TIP Soak wooden skewers in water for at least 30 minutes.

**TIP Refrigerate leftover aïoli in a covered container up to 3 days. Use as a spread for sandwiches or dip for vegetable or chips.

FOR 24 SERVINGS In Step 2 use 1 teaspoon salt, in Step 3 use twenty-four 6-inch skewers, in Step 4 use ½ teaspoon salt.

PER SERVING *174 cal., 15 g fat (2 g sat. fat), 26 mg chol., 107 mg sodium, 1 g carb., 0 g fiber, 9 g pro.*

Sausage Bites

The aroma of this trio of sausages simmering in a sweet and warmly spiced sauce is a wonderful way to welcome guests to your home. For convenience, the sausages can be prepared and kept warm in a slow cooker.

1. In an extra-large saucepan combine barbecue sauce, marmalade, dry mustard, and allspice. Cook and stir over medium-high heat until bubbly.

2. Stir in bratwurst, kielbasa, and smoked sausage links. Cook, covered, over medium-low heat for 20 minutes or until heated through, stirring occasionally.

SLOW COOKER DIRECTIONS For 20 servings, in a 3½- or 4-quart slow cooker combine barbecue sauce, marmalade, dry mustard, and allspice. Stir in bratwurst, kielbasa, and smoked sausage links. Cover and cook on high-heat setting for 2½ to 3 hours. Serve immediately or keep warm, covered, on low-heat setting up to 2 hours. For 40 servings, use a 5- to 6-quart slow cooker.

PER SERVING *206 cal., 13 g fat (5 g sat. fat), 27 mg chol., 609 mg sodium, 16 g carb., 0 g fiber, 6 g pro.*

START TO FINISH **30 minutes**

20 servings	ingredients	40 servings
1½ cups	barbecue sauce	3 cups
⅔ cup	orange marmalade	1⅓ cups
½ tsp.	dry mustard	1 tsp.
⅛ tsp.	ground allspice	¼ tsp.
12 oz.	cooked bratwurst, cut into ½-inch slices	24 oz.
12 oz.	cooked kielbasa, cut diagonally into ½-inch slices	24 oz.
8 oz.	cooked small smoked sausage links	16 oz.

Caribbean Cocktail Sausages

Jamaican jerk seasoning, lime, ginger, garlic, and a dash of hot pepper sauce give these snappy sausages tropical flavor.

1. In a 1½-quart slow cooker combine cocktail wieners, pineapple preserves, lime peel, lime juice, jerk seasoning, ginger, garlic, and hot pepper sauce. Cover and cook on low-heat setting for 4 hours. Serve immediately or keep warm, covered, on warm setting or low-heat setting up to 2 hours. Serve sausages with wooden picks.

FOR 24 SERVINGS Use a 3- to 4-quart slow cooker.

PER SERVING *194 cal., 10 g fat (4 g sat. fat), 24 mg chol., 421 mg sodium, 21 g carb., 0 g fiber, 5 g pro.*

PREP 15 minutes
SLOW COOK 4 hours (low)

12 servings	ingredients	24 servings
one 16-oz. pkg.	cocktail wieners or small, cooked smoked sausage links	two 16-oz. pkg.
one 12-oz. jar	pineapple preserves	two 12-oz. jars
½ tsp.	finely shredded lime peel	1 tsp.
1 Tbsp.	lime juice	2 Tbsp.
1 tsp.	Jamaican jerk seasoning	2 tsp.
1 tsp.	ground ginger	2 tsp.
2 cloves	garlic, minced	4 cloves
few dashes	bottled hot pepper sauce	⅛ tsp.

Ham Sliders

Hot ham and cheese is always a hit. These make-ahead sandwiches provide substantial party fare as part of an appetizer buffet.

1. Preheat oven to 350°F. Lightly coat a 13×9×2-inch baking pan with nonstick cooking spray; set aside. In a small bowl combine 2 tablespoons melted butter, flour and jam, breaking up any large pieces of fruit; set aside.

2. Cut rolls in half horizontally. Lay roll bottoms, cut sides up, in prepared pan. Spread each roll bottom with 1 teaspoon of jam mixture. Divide ham and cheese evenly among the roll bottoms. Add roll tops.

3. For the topping, in a small saucepan melt the ¼ cup butter over medium heat. Remove from heat; stir in brown sugar, mustard, and Worcestershire sauce. Using a pastry brush, coat roll tops with topping. Sprinkle roll tops with poppy seeds.

4. Bake sliders for 20 minutes or until cheese is melted and sliders are heated through.

FOR 24 SERVINGS Use two 13×9×2-inch baking pans. In Step 1 use ¼ cup melted butter, in Step 3 use ½ cup butter.

TO MAKE AHEAD Once sliders have been assembled, but before topping is made, cover tightly with plastic wrap and refrigerate up to 24 hours. Just before baking, prepare topping. Brush and bake as above.

PER SERVING *274 cal., 13 g fat (7 g sat. fat), 45 mg chol., 655 mg sodium, 27 g carb., 1 g fiber, 12 g pro.*

PREP 15 minutes
BAKE 20 minutes at 350°F

12 servings	ingredients	24 servings
	Nonstick cooking spray	
2 Tbsp.	butter, melted	¼ cup
1 Tbsp.	all-purpose flour	2 Tbsp.
1 cup	pineapple-apricot jam, pineapple jam, or apricot jam	2 cups
12	dinner rolls	24
1½ lb.	very thinly sliced cooked ham	3 lb.
12 oz.	cheddar cheese, thinly sliced	24 oz.
¼ cup	butter	½ cup
2 Tbsp.	packed brown sugar	¼ cup
2 tsp.	yellow mustard	4 tsp.
1 tsp.	Worcestershire sauce	2 tsp.
½ to ¾ tsp.	poppy seeds	1 to 1½ tsp.

Pizza Meatballs

The flavors of a classic Italian pie—mushrooms, peppers, onions, sausage, and cheese—are wrapped up in these yummy meatballs. Serve with warm pasta sauce for dipping.

1. Preheat oven to 350°F. Coat a large nonstick skillet with cooking spray; heat skillet over medium heat. Add mushrooms, green pepper, and onion. Cook for 5 to 8 minutes or until vegetables are tender, stirring frequently. Stir in garlic and set aside.

2. In a large bowl combine bread crumbs, egg white, Italian seasoning, and black pepper. Stir in mushroom mixture. Add turkey sausage, turkey breast, and cheese. Mix well.

3. Line a 15×10×1-inch baking pan with foil. Spray foil with cooking spray; set aside. Using wet hands, shape meat mixture into twenty-four 1½-inch meatballs. Place meatballs in the prepared pan. Bake for 20 minutes or until done (160°F).

4. In a small saucepan heat pasta sauce over medium heat, stirring occasionally. Serve with meatballs.

FOR 24 SERVINGS Use two 15×10×1-inch baking pans. Shape the meat mixture into forty-eight 1½-inch meatballs.

PER SERVING *122 cal., 4 g fat (2 g sat. fat), 29 mg chol., 225 mg sodium, 8 g carb., 1 g fiber, 12 g pro.*

PREP 25 minutes
BAKE 20 minutes at 350°F

12 servings	ingredients	24 servings
	Nonstick cooking spray	
1 cup	fresh cremini or button mushrooms, finely chopped	2 cups
½ cup	finely chopped green sweet pepper	1 cup
½ cup	finely chopped onion	1 cup
2 cloves	garlic, minced	4 cloves
¾ cup	soft whole wheat bread crumbs	1½ cups
1	egg white, lightly beaten	2
1½ tsp.	dried Italian seasoning, crushed	3 tsp.
⅛ tsp.	black pepper	¼ tsp.
8 oz.	uncooked bulk turkey sausage	16 oz.
8 oz.	ground turkey breast	16 oz.
1 cup	shredded reduced-fat Italian cheese blend	2 cups
1½ cups	purchased low-sodium pasta sauce	3 cups

Sweet-and-Sour-Glazed Chicken Sausage Bites

Lean chicken sausage lightens up the familiar party food of sausages glazed in a sweet and spicy chili sauce. Choose any flavor chicken sausage you like, including apple-Chardonnay, sun-dried tomato, or spicy jalapeño.

1. In a large saucepan heat oil over medium heat. Add onion, sweet pepper, and garlic; cook and stir for 3 minutes or until vegetables are tender.

2. Place vegetables and sausage slices in a 3½- or 4-quart slow cooker. In a small bowl stir together chili sauce, jelly, soy sauce, ginger, and crushed red pepper; pour over vegetables in slow cooker.

3. Cover and cook on low-heat setting for 3 to 4 hours or on high-heat setting for 1½ to 2 hours.

4. If using low-heat setting, turn to high-heat setting. In a small bowl combine cornstarch and the cold water. Stir cornstarch mixture into mixture in slow cooker. Cover and cook for 15 minutes more or until thickened. Serve immediately or keep warm, covered, on warm or low-heat setting up to 2 hours. Serve with toothpicks.

*TIP If desired, for 18 servings, substitute ½ teaspoon ground ginger in place of grated fresh ginger. For 36 servings, use 1 teaspoon ground ginger in place of grated fresh ginger.

FOR 36 SERVINGS Use a 5- to 6-quart slow cooker.

PER SERVING *125 cal., 3 g fat (1 g sat. fat), 47 mg chol., 65 mg sodium, 12 g carb., 1 g fiber, 12 g pro.*

PREP 20 minutes
SLOW COOK 3 hours (low) or 1½ hours (high) + 15 minutes (high)

18 servings	ingredients	36 servings
1 Tbsp.	olive oil	2 Tbsp.
½ cup	finely chopped onion	1 cup
⅓ cup	finely chopped red sweet pepper	⅔ cup
3 cloves	garlic, minced	6 cloves
three 12-oz. pkg.	apple-Chardonnay, sun-dried tomato, spicy jalapeño, and/or other cooked chicken sausage links, cut diagonally into ¾-inch slices	six 12-oz. pkg.
⅔ cup	chili sauce	1⅓ cups
⅔ cup	apple jelly	1⅓ cups
2 Tbsp.	soy sauce	4 Tbsp.
2 tsp.	grated fresh ginger*	4 tsp.
¼ tsp.	crushed red pepper	½ tsp.
¼ tsp.	cornstarch	½ tsp.
¼ tsp.	cold water	½ tsp.

Bourbon-Molasses-Glazed Chicken Wings

Pure maple syrup is pricey, but there is no substitute for the flavor it imparts to these tasty Southern-style wings.

PREP 30 minutes
MARINATE 1 hour
BAKE 50 minutes at 375°F

12 servings	ingredients	24 servings
24 (about 2½ lb.)	chicken wing pieces*	48 (about 5 lb.)
½ cup	Dijon mustard	1 cup
½ cup	pure maple syrup	1 cup
3 Tbsp.	cider vinegar	6 Tbsp.
3 Tbsp.	molasses	6 Tbsp.
2 Tbsp.	Asian chili sauce	¼ cup
2 Tbsp.	bourbon	¼ cup
2 tsp.	soy sauce	4 tsp.
	Nonstick cooking spray	
	Freshly ground black pepper	

1. Place chicken wing pieces in a resealable plastic bag set in a shallow dish.

2. For marinade, stir together mustard, maple syrup, vinegar, molasses, chili sauce, bourbon, and soy sauce. Pour over chicken wings. Seal bag; turn to coat chicken wings. Marinate in the refrigerator for 1 to 4 hours.

3. Preheat oven to 375°F. Line a shallow roasting pan with foil; lightly coat foil with cooking spray. Drain chicken wings, reserving marinade. Arrange wings in a single layer in prepared pan; sprinkle with pepper.

4. Bake for 30 minutes, spooning reserved marinade over wings twice. Turn wings over; spoon additional marinade over wings. Bake for 20 minutes more or until tender and no longer pink, spooning marinade over wings after 10 minutes. Discard any remaining marinade.

*TIP If you can't find chicken drummettes or chicken wing pieces, buy whole chicken wings, then cut off and discard the tips and cut the wings at the joint.

FOR 24 SERVINGS Use two shallow roasting pans.

PER SERVING *148 cal., 6 g fat (2 g sat. fat), 31 mg chol., 338 mg sodium, 13 g carb., 0 g fiber, 8 g pro.*

Pineapple Teriyaki Wings

For fresh presentation, serve these Polynesian-style wings on thinly sliced pineapple ring quarters. To save time, look for cored and prepared fresh pineapple in the produce section of supermarkets.

1. In an extra-large skillet heat oil over medium-high heat. Add chicken wing pieces; cook about 10 minutes or until browned on both sides. Drain off fat.

2. Meanwhile, for sauce, in a small bowl combine soy sauce, sake, pineapple juice, honey, ginger, and garlic. Pour sauce over chicken wing pieces.

3. Bring to boiling; reduce heat. Simmer, covered, for 5 minutes. Simmer, uncovered, for 10 to 15 minutes more or until chicken is no longer pink and sauce is slightly thickened, stirring occasionally. Transfer to a serving platter. Garnish with green onion.

PER SERVING *167 cal., 10 g fat (2 g sat. fat), 39 mg chol., 422 mg sodium, 5 g carb., 0 g fiber, 10 g pro.*

START TO FINISH **30 minutes**

12 servings	ingredients	24 servings
2 Tbsp.	vegetable oil	¼ cup
24 (about 2½ lb.)	chicken wing pieces (see tip, page 14)	48 (about 5 lb.)
½ cup	reduced-sodium soy sauce	1 cup
½ cup	sake or dry white wine	1 cup
⅓ cup	unsweetened pineapple juice	⅔ cup
2 Tbsp.	honey	¼ cup
2 Tbsp.	thinly sliced, peeled fresh ginger	¼ cup
1 clove	garlic, thinly sliced	2 cloves
2 Tbsp.	thinly sliced green onion strips	¼ cup

Rio Grande Dip

Creamy refried beans provide the base for this warm Mexican-style dip flavored with sausage, Monterey Jack cheese, salsa, and green chiles. Perfect for scooping!

PREP 20 minutes
SLOW COOK 3 hours (low)

24 servings	ingredients	48 servings
4 oz.	uncooked Italian turkey sausage links,* casings removed if needed	8 oz.
½	small onion, finely chopped	1
one 15-oz. can	reduced-fat refried black beans	two 15-oz. cans
¾ cup (3 oz.)	shredded reduced-fat Monterey Jack cheese	1½ cups (6 oz.)
¾ cup	bottled salsa	1½ cups
half 4-oz. can	diced green chiles, undrained	one 4-oz. can
2 Tbsp.	shredded reduced-fat Monterey Jack cheese (optional)	¼ cup
one 9-oz. bag	scoop-shape baked tortilla chips	two 9-oz. bags

1. In a medium skillet crumble sausage and cook with onion over medium-high heat until meat is browned, stirring to break up sausage as it cooks. Drain off fat. Transfer meat mixture to a 1½-quart slow cooker. Stir in refried beans, the ¾ cup cheese, the salsa, and chiles.

2. Cover and cook on low-heat setting for 3 to 4 hours. If no heat setting is available, cook for 3 to 4 hours.

3. Stir well before serving. Serve immediately or keep warm, covered, on warm or low-heat setting (if available) up to 2 hours. If desired, sprinkle with the 2 tablespoons cheese. Serve dip with tortilla chips.

*TIP If you can't find uncooked Italian turkey sausage links, for 24 servings, combine 4 ounces ground turkey with ¾ teaspoon Italian seasoning and ½ teaspoon paprika. For 48 servings, combine 8 ounces ground turkey with 1½ teaspoons Italian seasoning and 1 teaspoon paprika.

FOR 48 SERVINGS Use a 3- to 4½-quart slow cooker. In Step 1 use 1½ cups cheese.

PER SERVING *76 cal., 2 g fat (1 g sat. fat), 5 mg chol., 258 mg sodium, 12 g carb., 2 g fiber, 4 g pro.*

Swiss-Artichoke Dip

Some version of creamy artichoke dip is on the spread at nearly every gathering—a testament to its appeal. This version couldn't be easier— just stir together the artichokes, cheese, dried tomatoes, and seasonings in a slow cooker and let it do its magic. Serve with crackers.

1. In a 1½-quart slow cooker combine artichoke hearts, cream cheese, Swiss cheese, dried tomatoes, mayonnaise, milk, dried onion, and garlic.

2. Cover and cook on low-heat setting for 2½ to 3 hours or on high-heat setting for 1½ hours. If no heat setting is available, cook for 1½ hours.

3. Stir before serving. Serve dip with crackers.

*TIP This recipe calls for processed Swiss cheese because it melts smoothly; regular Swiss cheese will work also. The dip will have a more stretchy, less creamy texture yet taste just as good.

FOR 24 SERVINGS Use a 3- to 4½-quart slow cooker.

PER ¼ CUP DIP *113 cal., 10 g fat (4 g sat. fat), 22 mg chol., 173 mg sodium, 3 g carb., 1 g fiber, 3 g pro.*

PREP 15 minutes
SLOW COOK 2½ hours (low) or 1½ hours (high)

12 servings	ingredients	24 servings
one 8- to 9-oz. pkg.	frozen artichoke hearts, thawed and chopped	two 8- to 9-oz. pkg.
6 oz.	cream cheese, cut up	12 oz.
2 oz.	processed Swiss cheese slices, torn into small pieces*	4 oz.
¼ cup	snipped dried tomatoes (not oil packed)	½ cup
¼ cup	mayonnaise	½ cup
¼ cup	milk	½ cup
1 tsp.	dried minced onion	2 tsp.
1 clove	garlic, minced	2 cloves
	Crackers or toasted baguette slices	

Cheese and Almond Guacamole

Here's a hint for getting the best avocadoes: Buy them unripe, when they are still very firm and resist bruising and blemishing. Let them ripen and soften on the counter for a few days. When you open them, the flesh will be flawless.

1. In a large bowl combine avocados, onion, serrano peppers, almonds, chopped cilantro, lime juice, and salt; mash slightly with a fork, keeping the mixture chunky. Fold in goat cheese. Spoon guacamole into a serving bowl. Serve at once, or cover surface directly with plastic wrap and chill up to 6 hours.

2. Serve with carrot sticks, jicama strips, flatbread rounds, and/or pita chips and, if desired, lime wedges and cilantro sprigs.

*TIP Because chile peppers contain volatile oils that can burn skin and eyes, avoid direct contact with them as much as possible. When working with chile peppers, wear plastic or rubber gloves. If bare hands touch peppers, wash hands and nails well with soap and warm water.

PER ¼ CUP DIP *183 cal., 16 g fat (5 g sat. fat), 13 mg chol., 268 mg sodium, 8 g carb., 5 g fiber, 6 g pro.*

START TO FINISH 20 minutes

10 servings	ingredients	20 servings
4 medium	avocados, halved, seeded, peeled and coarsely chopped	8 medium
½ cup (1 medium)	chopped red onion	1 cup (1 large)
2	fresh serrano peppers,* halved, seeded (if desired), and finely chopped	4
½ cup	sliced almonds, toasted and coarsely chopped (see tip, page 24)	1 cup
⅓ cup	chopped fresh cilantro	⅔ cup
2 Tbsp.	fresh lime juice	¼ cup
¾ tsp.	salt	1½ tsp.
¾ cup	crumbled goat cheese or feta cheese	1½ cups
	Carrot sticks, jicama strips, flatbread rounds, and/or pita chips	
	Lime wedges and cilantro sprigs (optional)	

Artichoke Spread

It's always good to have something light and healthful on an appetizer spread as an option to the rich foods. This white bean and artichoke dip served with veggies fills the bill.

1. In a large food processor combine beans, artichoke hearts, garlic, lemon peel, lemon juice, salt, and cayenne pepper. Cover and process until nearly smooth, stopping to scrape down sides as necessary.

2. Transfer bean mixture to a serving bowl; stir in the thinly sliced green onion. Serve immediately or cover and chill for up to 2 days. If chilled, let stand at room temperature for 30 minutes before serving.

3. To serve, garnish with sliced green onion tops. Serve with cut-up vegetables.

PER 2 TABLESPOONS SPREAD *43 cal., 0 g fat, 0 mg chol., 57 mg sodium, 8 g carb., 3 g fiber, 2 g pro.*

START TO FINISH 15 minutes

16 servings	ingredients	32 servings
one 15-oz. can	no-salt-added cannellini beans (white kidney beans), rinsed and drained	2 15-oz. cans
one 9-oz. pkg.	frozen artichoke hearts, thawed and well drained	two 9-oz. pkg.
1 clove	garlic, quartered	2 cloves
1 tsp.	finely shredded lemon peel	2 tsp.
1 Tbsp.	lemon juice	2 Tbsp.
⅛ tsp.	salt	¼ tsp.
⅛ tsp.	cayenne pepper	¼ tsp.
1	green onion, thinly sliced	2
1 Tbsp.	sliced green onion tops	2 Tbsp.
8 cups	assorted vegetables, such as carrot sticks, celery sticks, cucumber slices, red sweet pepper strips, cauliflower florets, and/or broccoli florets	16 cups

Cannellini Salad-Topped Crostini

Tossed with cooked and cooled pasta (such as small shells, bowties, or mini-penne), cannellini salad can also be served a summery side dish or light main dish.

1. Preheat oven to 425°F. Using a serrated knife, cut bread diagonally into about 20 slices. Arrange bread slices on two large baking sheets. If desired, brush bread lightly with oil. Bake for 8 to 10 minutes or until light brown, turning once.

2. Meanwhile, in a medium bowl combine beans, tomatoes, zucchini, green onion, the 2 tablespoons oil, the vinegar, and mustard. Season to taste with salt and black pepper. Spoon salad onto toasted bread slices. Sprinkle with herbs.

TO MAKE AHEAD Prepare as directed in Step 1; cool bread. Transfer to an airtight container; cover. Store at room temperature for up to 24 hours. To serve, preheat oven to 425°F. Arrange bread slices on baking sheets. Bake about 3 minutes or just until crisp. Continue as directed in Step 2.

FOR 40 SERVINGS In Step 1 cut each loaf into 20 slices and bake in batches. In Step 2 use ¼ cup oil.

PER SERVING *58 cal., 1 g fat (0 g sat. fat), 0 mg chol., 140 mg sodium, 8 g carb., 1 g fiber, 2 g pro.*

PREP 15 minutes
BAKE 8 minutes at 425°F

20 servings	ingredients	40 servings
one 8-oz. loaf	baguette-style French bread	two 8-oz. loaves
	Olive oil (optional)	
one 15-oz. can	cannellini beans (white kidney beans), rinsed and drained	two 15-oz. cans
¼ cup	coarsely chopped grape tomatoes	½ cup
¼ cup	shredded zucchini, carrot, or red sweet pepper	½ cup
2 Tbsp.	chopped green onion	¼ cup
2 Tbsp.	olive oil	¼ cup
2 tsp.	red wine vinegar	4 tsp.
½ tsp.	coarse ground mustard	1 tsp.
	Salt	
	Cracked black pepper	
	Fresh marjoram, thyme, or oregano sprigs	

Spicy Shrimp Nachos

The sweetness of the mango and spiciness from the Jamaican jerk seasoning adds a whole new dimension to this classic Mexican snack.

1. Preheat broiler. For salsa, in a bowl stir together mango, sweet pepper, onion, and chile pepper; set aside. In a large bowl stir together brown sugar and jerk seasoning. Add shrimp and toss to coat. Coat a large skillet with cooking spray. Heat over medium-high heat. Add half the shrimp at a time to the pan. Cook for 1 to 2 minutes each side or until shrimp are opaque. Remove and set aside. If desired, coarsely chop shrimp.

2. Spread tortilla chips on a broiler-safe platter or baking sheet. Top with shrimp and salsa. Sprinkle with cheese. Broil 4 inches from heat for 1 to 2 minutes or until heated through and cheese is melted.

PER SERVING *283 cal., 12 g fat (4 g sat. fat), 99 mg chol., 507 mg sodium, 27 g carb., 2 g fiber, 17 g pro.*

PREP 30 minutes
BROIL 1 minute

8 servings	ingredients	16 servings
1 cup	mango, seeded, peeled, and chopped	2 cups
1 medium	red sweet pepper, chopped	2 medium
2 Tbsp.	finely chopped red onion	4 Tbsp.
1	fresh jalapeño, seeded and finely chopped (see tip, page 19)	2
2 Tbsp.	packed brown sugar	¼ cup
2 Tbsp.	Jamaican jerk seasoning	¼ cup
1 lb.	peeled, deveined uncooked shrimp	2 lb.
	Nonstick cooking spray	
8 cups (8 oz.)	tortilla chips	16 cups (16 oz.)
4 oz. (1 cup)	Monterey Jack cheese with jalapeño peppers or Monterey Jack cheese, shredded	8 oz. (2 cups)

Pimiento Cheese

This nostalgic Southern-style spread (affectionately referred to as "the caviar of the South") has experienced a renaissance in popularity in the last few years.

1. In a large bowl stir together cheese, mayonnaise, pimiento, Worcestershire, mustard, and garlic powder, mashing mixture with the back of a spoon as you mix (spread will be chunky). Transfer to a serving bowl. Cover with plastic wrap and chill for 4 to 24 hours. Serve as a spread with crackers.

PER SERVING *137 cal., 13 g fat (5 g sat. fat), 23 mg chol., 169 mg sodium, 1 g carb., 0 g fiber, 5 g pro.*

JALAPEÑO CHEESE For 18 or 36 servings, prepare as above, except omit the pimiento and mustard. Substitute Colby and Monterey Jack cheese for the cheddar cheese. For 18 servings, stir one 4-ounce can diced jalapeño peppers, drained, into the cheese mixture. For 36 servings, use two 4-ounce cans diced jalapeño peppers.

PREP 10 minutes
CHILL 4 hours

18 servings	ingredients	36 servings
1½ cups (12 oz.)	shredded cheddar cheese	3 cups (24 oz.)
⅔ cup	mayonnaise	1⅓ cups
one 4-oz. jar	sliced pimiento, drained and chopped	two 4-oz. jars
1 tsp.	Worcestershire sauce	2 tsp.
1 tsp.	yellow mustard	2 tsp.
¼ tsp.	garlic powder	½ tsp.
	Assorted crackers	

Sweet-and-Hot Nuts

These sweet and spicy nuts are very simple to prepare (in a slow cooker) and can be made up to 3 weeks ahead of serving.

1. Place nuts in a 2- to 3½-quart slow cooker. In a small bowl combine sugar, butter, ginger, salt, cinnamon, cloves, and cayenne pepper. Add butter mixture to slow cooker; toss to coat nuts.

2. Cover and cook on low-heat setting for 2 hours, stirring after 1 hour. Stir nuts again. Spread in a single layer on buttered foil; let cool for at least 1 hour. (Nuts may appear soft after cooking but will crisp upon cooling.) Store in a tightly covered container at room temperature up to 3 weeks.

*TIP To toast whole nuts or large pieces, spread them in a shallow pan. Bake at 350°F for 5 to 10 minutes, shaking the pan once or twice. Toast coconut in the same way, watching closely to avoid burning. Toast finely chopped or ground nuts or sesame seeds in a dry skillet over medium heat. Stir often to prevent burning.

**TIP To toast hazelnuts, spread nuts in a single layer in a shallow baking pan. Bake in a 350°F oven for 10 to 15 minutes or until light golden brown, watching carefully and stirring once or twice. To remove the papery skin from hazelnuts, rub the nuts with a clean dish towel.

FOR 44 SERVINGS Use a 5- to 6-quart slow cooker.

PER SERVING *147 cal., 13 g fat (3 g sat. fat), 7 mg chol., 73 mg sodium, 8 g carb., 2 g fiber, 3 g pro.*

PREP 15 minutes
SLOW COOK 2 hours (low)
COOL 1 hour

22 servings	ingredients	44 servings
1 cup	whole cashews	2 cups
1 cup	whole almonds, toasted*	2 cups
1 cup	pecan halves, toasted*	2 cups
1 cup	hazelnuts, toasted and skins removed**	2 cups
½ cup	sugar	1 cup
⅓ cup	butter, melted	⅔ cup
1 tsp.	ground ginger	2 tsp.
½ tsp.	salt	1 tsp.
½ tsp.	ground cinnamon	1 tsp.
¼ tsp.	ground cloves	½ tsp.
¼ tsp.	cayenne pepper	½ tsp.

Lemon-Zested Snacker Mix

This addictive snack mix is a crunch-inducing blend of whole-grain cereal, pita chips, nuts, and pumpkin seeds flavored with ranch dressing mix, dill, rosemary, and lemon.

1. Lightly coat a 2- to 3½-quart slow cooker with cooking spray. In prepared slow cooker combine cereal, pita chips, walnuts, pumpkin seeds, salad dressing mix, dill weed, and rosemary. Drizzle mixture with oil, tossing gently to blend.

2. Cover and cook on low-heat setting for 2½ hours, stirring every 40 minutes, or on high-heat setting for 80 minutes, stirring every 20 minutes.

3. Sprinkle lemon peel over mix, tossing gently to blend. Spread mix in an even layer on a large baking sheet; cool completely. Store in an airtight container for up to 2 weeks.

FOR 24 SERVINGS Use a 5- to 6-quart slow cooker.

PER SERVING *107 cal., 5 g fat (1 g sat. fat), 0 mg chol., 209 mg sodium, 15 g carb., 2 g fiber, 2 g pro.*

PREP 15 minutes
SLOW COOK 2½ hours (low) or 80 minutes (high)

12 servings	ingredients	24 servings
	Nonstick cooking spray	
2½ cups	bite-size multigrain or wheat square cereal	5 cups
1 cup	plain pita chips, broken into bite-sizes pieces	2 cups
⅓ cup	chopped walnuts	⅔ cup
2 Tbsp.	pumpkin seeds (pepitas)	¼ cup
half 1-oz. packet	dry ranch salad dressing mix	one 1-oz. packet
1 Tbsp.	dried dill weed	2 Tbsp.
½ tsp.	dried rosemary, crushed	1 tsp.
1 Tbsp.	olive oil	2 Tbsp.
1½ tsp.	finely shredded lemon peel	1 Tbsp.

Onion and Garlic Macadamia Nuts

Rich, buttery-tasting macadamia nuts are skillet-roasted with spices and just a hint of sugar for a very special snack.

1. In a large skillet heat oil over medium heat for 1 to 2 minutes or until very hot. Carefully add parsley, onion salt, sugar, lemon juice, and garlic powder, stirring until combined. Add macadamia nuts.

2. Cook and stir for 5 minutes. Drain nuts on paper towels; cool.

PER SERVING *274 cal., 29 g fat (5 g sat. fat), 0 mg chol., 402 mg sodium, 5 g carb., 3 g fiber, 3 g pro.*

PREP 10 minutes
COOK 5 minutes

12 servings	ingredients	24 servings
3 Tbsp.	olive oil	6 Tbsp.
1 Tbsp.	dried parsley flakes	2 Tbsp.
1 Tbsp.	onion salt	2 Tbsp.
1½ tsp.	sugar	1 Tbsp.
1½ tsp.	lemon juice	1 Tbsp.
¾ tsp.	garlic powder	1½ tsp.
3 cups (14 oz.)	macadamia nuts	6 cups (28 oz.)

Pink Lemonade Slush

This frosty pretty-in-pink drink is perfect for a summer party. It freezes for 4 hours ahead of serving time so it can be ready and waiting when guests start to arrive.

1. In a blender combine half the water, one can lemonade concentrate, and one package frozen raspberries in syrup; add half the ice. Cover and blend until smooth and slushy, stopping to scrape down sides as necessary. Transfer to a 6-quart freezer container. Repeat with remaining water, lemonade concentrate, raspberries, and ice. Transfer to another 6-quart freezer container. Cover and freeze about 4 hours or until firm.

2. To serve, scoop frozen lemonade mixture into glasses. Slowly pour carbonated beverage over frozen mixture; stir gently.

FOR 40 SERVINGS In Step 1 use four 6-quart freezer containers.

PER 8-OUNCE SERVING *157 cal., 0 g fat, 0 mg chol., 33 mg sodium, 41 g carb., 1 g fiber, 0 g pro.*

PREP 15 minutes
FREEZE 4 hours

20 servings	ingredients	40 servings
2½ cups	cold water	5 cups
two 12-oz. cans	frozen pink lemonade concentrate	four 12-oz. cans
two 10-oz. pkg.	frozen red raspberries in syrup	four 10-oz. pkg.
3 cups	ice cubes	6 cups
10 cups	lemon-lime carbonated beverage	20 cups

Creamy Berry Citrus Punch

Two flavors of sherbet—orange and raspberry—add color, flavor, and creaminess to this pastel party punch.

1. In a punch bowl or extra-large pitcher stir together limeade and cranberry juice. Cover and chill until ready to serve, up to 24 hours.

2. Just before serving, top with scoops of orange and raspberry sherbet. Slowly pour carbonated beverage down the side of the bowl. Stir gently to muddle. Add desired fruit.

PER SERVING *133 cal., 0 g fat, 0 mg chol., 52 mg sodium, 33 g carb., 1 g fiber, 0 g pro.*

START TO FINISH 15 minutes

16 servings	ingredients	32 servings
2 cups	refrigerated limeade	4 cups
2 cups	white cranberry juice	4 cups
1 pint	orange sherbet	2 pints
1 pint	raspberry sherbet	2 pints
one 2-liter bottle	lemon-lime carbonated beverage, chilled	two 2-liter bottles
	Lime slices, lemon slices, and/or orange slices	

CHAPTER 2

Poultry

Versatile and budget-friendly poultry is a popular pick for dinner. These chicken and turkey dishes offer a variety of flavors to please any palate.

34

55

66

Cilantro Chicken with Peanuts

Truly a flash in the pan, this quick chicken served over crunchy napa cabbage is infused with Asian flavors—ginger, garlic, green onions, soy, sesame, cilantro, and lime.

1. In a large heavy skillet heat peanut oil over high heat. Add chicken; cook and stir for 2 minutes. Add peanuts, ginger, and garlic; cook and stir about 3 minutes or until no pink remains in chicken.

2. Add green onions, soy sauce, rice vinegar, and sesame oil to skillet. Cook and stir for 2 minutes. Remove from heat. Stir in the 1 cup cilantro.

3. To serve, spoon the chicken over cabbage. If desired, garnish with additional cilantro and lime wedges.

*TIP If desired, use hot cooked brown rice in place of the napa cabbage. For 4 servings, use 2 cups rice. For 8 servings, use 4 cups rice.

FOR 8 SERVINGS In Step 2 stir in the 2 cups cilantro.

PER SERVING *222 cal., 9 g fat (2 g sat. fat), 66 mg chol., 362 mg sodium, 7 g carb., 2 g fiber, 30 g pro.*

START TO FINISH 25 minutes

4 servings	ingredients	8 servings
2 tsp.	peanut oil	4 tsp.
1 lb.	skinless, boneless chicken breast halves, cut into 1-inch pieces	2 lb.
¼ cup	honey-roasted peanuts	½ cup
2 tsp.	minced fresh ginger	4 tsp.
4 cloves	garlic, minced	8 cloves
¼ cup (2)	sliced green onions	½ cup (4)
1 Tbsp.	soy sauce	2 Tbsp.
2 tsp.	rice vinegar	4 tsp.
1 tsp.	toasted sesame oil	2 tsp.
1 cup	fresh cilantro leaves	2 cups
4 cups	finely shredded napa cabbage*	8 cups
	Fresh cilantro (optional)	
	Lime wedges (optional)	

Feta-Stuffed Chicken Breasts

If you'd like, stuff the chicken breasts a few hours ahead of serving time. Cover them tightly with plastic wrap and refrigerate for 2 or 3 hours before seasoning and cooking.

1. Place tomatoes in a bowl. Add enough boiling water to cover the tomatoes. Let stand for 10 minutes. Drain and pat dry; set aside.

2. Meanwhile, using a sharp knife, cut a pocket in each chicken breast half by cutting horizontally through the thickest portion to, but not through, the opposite side. Set chicken aside.

3. In a bowl combine feta cheese, cream cheese, basil, and tomatoes. Spoon about 1 rounded tablespoon of the feta filling into the pocket in each chicken breast half. If necessary, secure openings with wooden toothpicks. Sprinkle chicken with pepper.

4. In a large nonstick skillet heat oil over medium-high heat. Cook chicken in the hot oil for 12 to 14 minutes or until no pink remains (165°F), turning once. (Reduce heat to medium if chicken browns too quickly.) If desired, drizzle vinaigrette over greens and serve with chicken.

*TIP If desired, for 4 servings, use ½ teaspoon dried basil in place of the 2 teaspoons snipped fresh basil. For 8 servings, use 1 teaspoon dried basil in place of the 4 teaspoons snipped fresh basil.

PER SERVING *168 cal., 5 g fat (2 g sat. fat), 75 mg chol., 221 mg sodium, 1 g carb., 0 g fiber, 29 g pro.*

START TO FINISH **30 minutes**

4 servings	ingredients	8 servings
1 Tbsp.	snipped dried tomatoes (not oil-packed)	2 Tbsp.
4 (1 to 1½ lb. total)	skinless, boneless chicken breast halves	8 (2 to 3 lb. total)
¼ cup	crumbled feta cheese	½ cup
2 Tbsp.	fat-free cream cheese, softened	¼ cup
2 tsp.	snipped fresh basil*	4 tsp.
⅛ tsp.	black pepper	¼ tsp.
1 tsp.	olive oil	2 tsp.
	Bottled vinaigrette (optional)	
	Salad greens (optional)	

Herbed Chicken, Orzo, and Zucchini

When there's an abundance of zucchini and summer squash in the garden—and time is of the essence—make this 20-minute one-dish meal.

1. Prepare orzo according to package directions; drain. Return to hot saucepan. Cover; keep warm.

2. Meanwhile, sprinkle chicken with basil. In a large skillet heat 1 tablespoon of the oil over medium-high heat. Add chicken; cook about 12 minutes or until no pink remains (165°F), turning once. (Reduce heat to medium if chicken browns too quickly.) Remove chicken from skillet. Add zucchini and/or squash to skillet; cook and stir for 3 minutes or until crisp-tender.

3. Add orzo, vinegar, the remaining oil, and the snipped dill to skillet. Stir to combine.

4. Serve chicken with orzo and zucchini. If desired, sprinkle with dill sprigs.

FOR 8 SERVINGS In Step 2 use 2 tablespoons of the oil.

PER SERVING *390 cal., 12 g fat (2 g sat. fat), 66 mg chol., 233 mg sodium, 35 g carb., 3 g fiber, 33 g pro.*

START TO FINISH **20 minutes**

4 servings	ingredients	8 servings
1 cup	dried orzo pasta	2 cups
four (1 to 1½ lb. total)	skinless, boneless chicken breast halves	eight (2 to 3 lb. total)
1 tsp.	dried basil, crushed	2 tsp.
3 Tbsp.	olive oil	6 Tbsp.
2 medium	zucchini and/or yellow summer squash, halved lengthwise and sliced	4 medium
2 Tbsp.	red wine vinegar	¼ cup
1 Tbsp.	snipped fresh dill	2 Tbsp.
	Fresh dill sprigs (optional)	

Maple-Glazed Chicken with Sweet Potatoes

Six simple ingredients are transformed into a tasty autumnal meal in less time than it takes to order and carry out a meal from a restaurant.

1. Prepare sweet potatoes according to microwave package directions.

2. Meanwhile, lightly coat chicken with steak seasoning and slice into ½-inch slices. In a large skillet melt butter over medium-high heat. Add chicken; cook for 5 to 6 minutes or until no longer pink, turning once. Remove chicken from skillet; cover and keep warm. Stir maple syrup into hot skillet; cook for 2 minutes more. Stir in green onions.

3. Divide chicken and sweet potatoes among dinner plates. Drizzle with maple syrup glaze.

PER SERVING *384 cal., 7 g fat (4 g sat. fat), 81 mg chol., 505 mg sodium, 50 g carb., 6 g fiber, 30 g pro.*

START TO FINISH **20 minutes**

4 servings	ingredients	8 servings
one 24-oz. pkg.	refrigerated mashed sweet potatoes	two 24-oz. pkg.
1 lb.	skinless, boneless chicken breast halves	2 lb.
2 tsp.	steak grilling seasoning blend, such as Montreal	4 tsp.
2 Tbsp.	butter	¼ cup
¼ cup	maple syrup	½ cup
½ cup (4)	sliced green onions	1 cup (8)

Glazed Chicken with Wilted Spinach

This colorful dish is full of fresh, crunchy textures from crisp apple and barely wilted spinach. Spinach tastes best—and is most nutritious—when it very lightly cooked.

1. For the ginger-apple glaze, in a small saucepan combine apple jelly, soy sauce, thyme, lemon peel, and ginger. Cook and stir just until jelly is melted. Remove ¼ cup of the glaze to use for the wilted spinach.

2. For a gas or charcoal grill, place chicken on the grill rack directly over medium heat. Cover and grill for 12 to 15 minutes or until chicken is no longer pink (165°F), turning once halfway through grilling and brushing frequently with the remaining glaze during the last 5 minutes of grilling. Remove chicken from grill; cover and keep warm.

3. Lightly coat a Dutch oven with cooking spray; heat Dutch oven over medium heat. Add apples, leek, and garlic; cook for 3 minutes, stirring occasionally. Stir in the reserved glaze and the apple juice. Bring to boiling. Add spinach; toss just until wilted. Remove from heat. Season to taste with salt and pepper.

4. Divide spinach among dinner plates. Slice chicken and place on top of spinach.

*TIP If desired, for 4 servings, substitute 1 teaspoon dried thyme, crushed, in place of the fresh thyme. For 8 servings, use 2 teaspoons dried thyme, crushed, in place of the fresh thyme.

FOR 8 SERVINGS In Step 1 remove ½ cup of the glaze to use for the wilted spinach.

PER SERVING 335 cal., 2 g fat (0 g sat. fat), 82 mg chol., 673 mg sodium, 44 g carb., 4 g fiber, 36 g pro.

PREP 20 minutes   GRILL 12 minutes

4 servings	ingredients	8 servings
½ cup	apple jelly	1 cup
2 Tbsp.	soy sauce	¼ cup
1 Tbsp.	snipped fresh thyme*	2 Tbsp.
1 tsp.	finely shredded lemon peel	2 tsp.
1 tsp.	grated fresh ginger	2 tsp.
1¼ lb.	skinless, boneless chicken breast halves	2½ lb.
	Nonstick cooking spray	
2 cups	sliced apples	4 cups
⅓ cup	sliced leek or chopped onion	⅔ cup
2	cloves garlic, minced	4
2 Tbsp.	apple juice or chicken broth	¼ cup
one 10-oz. pkg.	fresh spinach	two 10-oz. pkg.
	Salt	
	Black pepper	

Thai Peanut Chicken

Serve this aromatic dish with hot cooked jasmine rice, which has a wonderful perfume and flavor.

1. In a medium saucepan whisk together coconut milk and peanut butter until nearly smooth. Whisk in broth, soy sauce, vinegar, brown sugar, sesame oil, curry paste, ginger, garlic, and cayenne pepper. Bring just to boiling over medium-high heat; reduce heat. Simmer, uncovered, for 15 minutes, stirring occasionally.

2. Preheat oven to 300°F. In a plastic bag combine flour, salt, and black pepper. If desired, remove skin from chicken. Add chicken pieces, one at a time, to flour mixture, shaking to coat.

3. In a large skillet cook chicken, half at a time, in hot oil until browned, turning occasionally. Transfer chicken to an ungreased 3-quart rectangular baking dish. Pour peanut butter sauce over chicken. Cover loosely with foil. Bake for 1 hour, occasionally spooning sauce over chicken. Uncover and bake 20 to 30 minutes more or until chicken is cooked through (175°F).

3. Transfer chicken to a serving platter. Skim fat from sauce in dish. Spoon some of the sauce over chicken. Sprinkle with cilantro. Pass remaining sauce and hot cooked rice.

FOR 8 SERVINGS Use two 3-quart baking dishes.

PER SERVING *901 cal., 62 g fat (29 g sat. fat), 139 mg chol., 1,211 mg sodium, 47 g carb., 5 g fiber, 42 g pro.*

PREP 40 minutes BAKE 1 hour 20 minutes at 300°F

4 servings	ingredients	8 servings
one 14-oz. can	unsweetened coconut milk	two 14-oz. cans
¼ cup	creamy peanut butter	½ cup
⅓ cup	chicken broth	⅔ cup
2 Tbsp.	soy sauce	¼ cup
2 Tbsp.	rice vinegar	¼ cup
1 Tbsp.	brown sugar	2 Tbsp.
1 Tbsp.	toasted sesame oil	2 Tbsp.
2 tsp.	red curry paste	4 tsp.
1 tsp.	grated fresh ginger	2 tsp.
1	clove garlic	2
⅛ to ¼ tsp.	cayenne pepper	¼ to ½ tsp.
½ cup	all-purpose flour	1 cup
½ tsp.	salt	1 tsp.
½ tsp.	black pepper	1 tsp.
4	chicken legs (thigh-drumstick piece)	8
2 Tbsp.	vegetable oil	¼ cup
2 Tbsp.	snipped fresh cilantro	¼ cup
2 cups	hot cooked rice	4 cups

Sesame Chicken Nuggets with Green Beans

For the crispest sesame-crusted chicken, allow plenty of space in the skillet while frying. Pieces that are crowded will become soggy.

1. Cut chicken into 1½-inch pieces. In a shallow dish combine flour, sesame seeds, pepper, and salt. Place eggs in another shallow dish. Dip chicken pieces into flour mixture, then into eggs, then into flour mixture again to coat. Set aside.

2. In a large skillet heat about ½ inch oil over medium-high heat. Add chicken pieces, half at a time, and cook for 4 to 5 minutes or until golden brown and cooked through (175°F). Using a slotted spoon, transfer to paper towels to drain.

3. Meanwhile, in a large skillet combine carrot, honey, vinegar, and the water. Bring to boiling. Stir in green beans. Add chicken; stir to coat. If desired, serve over hot cooked rice.

PER SERVING *520 cal., 26 g fat (4 g sat. fat), 201 mg chol., 747 mg sodium, 43 g carb., 4 g fiber, 29 g pro.*

PREP 25 minutes COOK 15 minutes

4 servings	ingredients	8 servings
1 lb.	skinless, boneless chicken thighs	2 lb.
½ cup	all-purpose flour	1 cup
⅓ cup	sesame seeds	⅔ cup
1 tsp.	black pepper	2 tsp.
½ tsp.	salt	1 tsp.
2	eggs, lightly beaten	4
	Vegetable oil	
1	large carrot, thinly sliced and coarsely chopped	2
⅓ cup	honey	⅔ cup
3 Tbsp.	cider vinegar	6 Tbsp.
1 Tbsp.	water	2 Tbsp.
one 14.5-oz. can	cut green beans, drained	two 14.5-oz. cans
	Hot cooked rice (optional)	

Lemon-Ginger Chicken Thighs

Bone-in chicken thighs are an economical choice when cooking for a large group—and they're delicious too. Poultry cooked on the bone turns out juicier and more flavorful than boneless.

START TO FINISH 35 minutes

4 servings	ingredients	8 servings
1	lemon	2
1 Tbsp.	grated fresh ginger	2 Tbsp.
½ tsp.	salt	1 tsp.
2 Tbsp.	honey	¼ cup
2 Tbsp.	water	¼ cup
1 Tbsp.	reduced-sodium soy sauce	2 Tbsp.
8	bone-in chicken thighs	16
2 tsp.	vegetable oil	4 tsp.
	Slivered green onions (optional)	
	Lemon wedges (optional)	

1. Finely shred peel from lemon then juice the lemon. In a small bowl combine lemon peel, ginger, and salt. In another small bowl combine lemon juice, honey, the water, and soy sauce.

2. Rub lemon peel mixture under the skin of chicken thighs. In an extra-large skillet heat oil over medium-high heat. Cook chicken, skin sides down, in hot oil for 7 minutes or until well browned. Turn chicken; add lemon juice mixture. Reduce heat. Cook, covered, for 14 to 18 minutes or until chicken is no longer pink (175°F).

3. Transfer chicken to dinner plates. If desired, skim fat from pan juices and drizzle juices over chicken. If desired, sprinkle with green onions and serve with lemon wedges.

PER SERVING *459 cal., 31 g fat (8 g sat. fat), 158 mg chol., 567 mg sodium, 12 g carb., 1 g fiber, 33 g pro.*

Chicken Dijonnaise

Serve this French-style dish with oven-roasted potatoes and steamed whole green beans.

1. Place each chicken breast half between two pieces of plastic wrap. Using the flat side of a meat mallet, pound chicken lightly to ¼-inch thickness. Remove plastic wrap. In a shallow dish stir together flour and pepper. Dip chicken into flour mixture, turning to coat.

2. In an extra-large skillet melt butter over medium heat. Add chicken; cook for 6 minutes or until chicken is no longer pink (165°), turning once. Transfer chicken to a serving platter, reserving drippings in skillet. Keep chicken warm.

3. For sauce, add green onion to the reserved drippings. Cook and stir over medium heat for 1 to 2 minutes or until tender. Stir in whipping cream, wine, and mustard. Cook and stir for 1 to 2 minutes or until smooth and slightly thickened.

4. Spoon sauce over chicken. If desired, snip fresh thyme to sprinkle leaves over chicken.

PER SERVING *298 cal., 16 g fat (8 g sat. fat), 110 mg chol., 208 mg sodium, 8 g carb., 1 g fiber, 28 g pro.*

START TO FINISH **30 minutes**

4 servings	ingredients	8 servings
four (1¼ to 1½ lb. total)	skinless, boneless chicken breast halves	eight (2½ to 3 lb. total)
¼ cup	all-purpose flour	½ cup
¼ tsp.	black pepper	½ tsp.
2 Tbsp.	butter	¼ cup
2 Tbsp.	chopped green onion	¼ cup
⅓ cup	whipping cream	⅔ cup
3 Tbsp.	dry white wine or chicken broth	6 Tbsp.
3 Tbsp.	Dijon mustard	6 Tbsp.
	Fresh thyme (optional)	

Fruited Chicken Salad

This whole-meal salad of peppery greens, chilled chicken, and ripe pears or apples—served with toast slathered with honey butter—is a fresh and creative way to plate rotisserie chicken.

START TO FINISH 30 minutes

4 servings	ingredients	8 servings
½ cup	crème fraîche or sour cream	1 cup
¼ cup	white wine vinegar	½ cup
3 to 4 Tbsp.	Dijon mustard	6 to 8 Tbsp.
2	cloves garlic, minced	4
½ tsp.	salt	1 tsp.
¼ tsp.	black pepper	½ tsp.
4 slices	Texas toast or sourdough bread, toasted	8 slices
2 to 4 Tbsp.	honey butter	6 to 8 Tbsp.
6 cups	arugula mix	12 cups
½ cup	lightly packed small fresh mint leaves	1 cup
2 Tbsp.	shredded fresh basil	¼ cup
one 2- to 2¼-lb.	purchased roasted chicken, quartered and chilled	two 2- to 2¼-lb.
2 cups	sliced pears and/or apples	4 cups

1. For dressing, in a small bowl whisk together crème fraîche, vinegar, mustard, garlic, salt, and pepper; set aside.

2. Spread toast slices with honey butter; divide among dinner plates. In a large bowl combine salad greens, mint, and basil. Divide greens among toast slices. Arrange chicken and pears and/or apples on greens. Drizzle with dressing.

TO MAKE-AHEAD Prepare dressing as directed in Step 1. Cover and chill up to 24 hours. Continue as directed.

PER SERVING 677 cal., 36 g fat (13 g sat. fat), 218 mg chol., 965 mg sodium, 37 g carb., 3 g fiber, 52 g pro.

Teriyaki Chicken

Remove the skin from the chicken before placing it in the slow cooker. Chicken skin gets crisp and delicious in the intense high heat of the oven, but doesn't take on that same quality when cooked in the moist, low-heat environment of a slow cooker.

1. Place chicken in a 3½- or 4-quart slow cooker. In a small bowl stir together soy sauce, sherry, the water, sesame oil, vinegar, ginger, and garlic. Pour soy mixture over chicken.

2. Cover and cook on low-heat setting for 5 to 6 hours or on high-heat setting for 2½ to 3 hours. Transfer chicken to a serving platter, reserving cooking liquid. Cover chicken with foil and keep warm.

3. Stir bok choy into cooking liquid; cover and let stand for 5 minutes. Transfer bok choy to the serving platter with chicken. Sprinkle chicken and bok choy with sesame seeds and, if desired, drizzle with some of the cooking liquid.

FOR 12 SERVINGS In Step 1 use a 5- to 6-quart slow cooker.

PER SERVING *253 cal., 10 g fat (2 g sat. fat), 92 mg chol., 513 mg sodium, 4 g carb., 1 g fiber, 32 g pro.*

PREP 20 minutes   SLOW COOK 5 hours (low) or 2½ hours (high)   STAND 5 minutes

6 servings	ingredients	12 servings
3 to 3½ lb.	meaty chicken pieces (breast halves, thighs, and drumsticks), skin removed	6 to 7 lb.
¼ cup	reduced-sodium soy sauce	½ cup
¼ cup	dry sherry	½ cup
¼ cup	water	½ cup
1 Tbsp.	toasted sesame oil	2 Tbsp.
1 Tbsp.	rice vinegar	2 Tbsp.
1 Tbsp.	grated fresh ginger	2 Tbsp.
2 cloves	garlic, minced	4 cloves
6 cups	sliced bok choy or shredded napa cabbage	12 cups
2 tsp.	toasted sesame seeds	4 tsp.

Pappardelle with Chicken and Peas

As simple as it is to put together, this chicken and pasta dish is company worthy. A splash of evaporated milk gives the sauce—made with flavorful Italian-style stewed tomatoes—lovely creaminess that only tastes decadent.

1. Cook noodles according to package directions, adding peas for the last 3 minutes of cooking time. Meanwhile, place tomatoes in a food processor or blender. Cover and process or blend until smooth; set aside.

2. In a large skillet heat oil over medium-high heat. Add chicken and onion; sprinkle with pepper. Cook for 2 to 4 minutes or just until chicken is cooked through and no pink remains.

3. Add broth and the pureed tomatoes to chicken in skillet. Bring to boiling; reduce heat. Boil gently, uncovered, for 2 minutes. Stir in evaporated milk; boil gently for 3 minutes more or until sauce thickens slightly.

4. Drain noodles and peas; transfer to warm serving bowls. Spoon chicken over noodles and peas. Top with Parmigiano-Reggiano cheese.

PER SERVING *329 cal., 6 g fat (1 g sat. fat), 71 mg chol., 419 mg sodium, 44 g carb., 5 g fiber, 25 g pro.*

PREP 10 minutes   COOK 10 minutes

4 servings	ingredients	8 servings
6 oz.	dried pappardelle or other wide egg noodles	12 oz.
1½ cups	shelled sweet peas or frozen peas	3 cups
half 14.5-oz. can	Italian-style stewed tomatoes, undrained	one 14.5-oz. can
2 tsp.	olive oil	4 tsp.
8 oz.	skinless, boneless chicken breast halves, cut into bite-size pieces	1 lb.
1 small	onion, cut into thin wedges	2 small
¼ tsp.	coarsely ground black pepper	½ tsp.
¼ cup	reduced-sodium chicken broth	½ cup
¼ cup	evaporated fat-free milk	½ cup
2 Tbsp.	freshly grated Parmigiano-Reggiano cheese	¼ cup

Sweet and Salty Chicken Salad

The highly appealing combo of sweet and salty flavors is the star of this peanut-sauced and stacked salad that's just right for a no-cook night.

1. Remove and discard skin and bones from chicken. Shred chicken into bite-size pieces. Cut pineapple into ¼-inch slices or spears. On each dinner plate arrange the pineapple, cabbage, chicken, apple, and grapes.

2. For dressing, in a small bowl whisk together stir-fry sauce and peanut butter until combined. If necessary, add enough water, 1 teaspoon at a time, to reach drizzling consistency. Drizzle stacked salads with dressing and sprinkle with crushed red pepper.

PER SERVING *529 cal., 19 g fat (5 g sat. fat), 123 mg chol., 998 mg sodium, 44 g carb., 5 g fiber, 45 g pro.*

START TO FINISH **30 minutes**

4 servings	ingredients	8 servings
one 2- to 2½-lb.	purchased roasted chicken	two 2- to 2½-lb.
1	fresh pineapple, peeled and quartered lengthwise	2
½	head napa cabbage, cut crosswise into 1-inch pieces	1
1 medium	Granny Smith apple, cut into thin wedges	2 medium
1 cup	green and/or red seedless grapes, halved	2 cups
½ cup	ginger-sesame stir-fry sauce	1 cup
¼ cup	creamy peanut butter	½ cup
	Water (optional)	
¼ tsp.	crushed red pepper	½ tsp.

Spicy Chicken Sausage Pasta and Greens

Sausage, pasta and greens is a classic Italian combination. The pleasantly bitter flavor of the greens complements the richness of the sausage and cheese—and the chewy pasta provides a palette for all of it.

START TO FINISH 30 minutes

4 servings	ingredients	8 servings
8 oz. (3 cups)	medium shell pasta	16 oz. (6 cups)
1 bunch (3 cups)	Broccolini, cut into 1-inch pieces	2 bunches (6 cups)
2 Tbsp.	olive oil	4 Tbsp.
one 12-oz.. pkg.	fully cooked spicy chicken sausage links, cut into ½-inch slices	two 12-oz. pkg.
1	small onion, coarsely chopped	2
3 cloves	garlic, minced	6 cloves
1 cup	reduced-sodium chicken broth	2 cups
½ tsp.	kosher salt	1 tsp.
¼ tsp.	black pepper	½ tsp.
1½ cups	arugula	3 cups
¼ cup	snipped fresh dill	½ cup
¼ cup	grated Parmesan cheese	½ cup
	Olive oil (optional)	
	Crushed red pepper (optional)	

1. In a Dutch oven cook pasta according to package directions, adding the Broccolini for the last 4 minutes of cooking time. Drain; rinse with cold water and drain again. Set aside.

2. In an extra-large skillet heat the 2 tablespoons oil over medium-high heat. Add chicken sausage, onion, and garlic. Cook, turning occasionally, for 3 minutes or until sausage is browned. Add pasta mixture, chicken broth, salt, and pepper. Heat through. Add arugula and dill. Remove from heat; toss to wilt greens.

3. Divide among shallow bowls. Sprinkle each serving with Parmesan cheese. If desired, drizzle with a little olive oil and sprinkle with crushed red pepper.

FOR 8 SERVINGS In Step 2 use 4 tablespoons olive oil.

PER SERVING 432 cal., 13 g fat (4 g sat. fat), 69 mg chol., 847 mg sodium, 52 g carb., 4 g fiber, 28 g pro.

Fresh Corn and Chicken Chowder

Instant mashed potato flakes are the surprise ingredient in this quick chowder that gives it such wonderful body.

1. In a Dutch oven combine chicken, corn, and broth. Bring to boiling; reduce heat. Simmer, covered, for 12 minutes or until no pink remains in chicken. Transfer chicken and corn to a cutting board.

2. Add ¼ cup of the sweet pepper to broth in Dutch oven. Stir in potato flakes and milk. Using two forks, shred chicken. Return chicken to Dutch oven.

3. Using a kitchen towel to hold hot corn, cut kernels from cobs leaving some corn in planks. Add corn to chowder in Dutch oven; heat through. Season to taste with salt and black pepper. Top servings with the remaining chopped sweet pepper. If desired, sprinkle with crushed red pepper.

FOR 8 SERVINGS In Step 2 add ½ cup of the sweet pepper to broth in Dutch oven.

PER SERVING *269 cal., 3 g fat (1 g sat. fat), 54 mg chol., 721 mg sodium, 33 g carb., 3 g fiber, 29 g pro.*

START TO FINISH **30 minutes**

4 servings	ingredients	8 servings
12 oz.	skinless, boneless chicken breast halves or chicken thighs	24 oz.
4	fresh ears sweet corn	8
one 32-oz. box	reduced-sodium chicken broth	two 32-oz. boxes
½ cup	chopped green sweet pepper	1 cup
1¼ cups	instant mashed potato flakes	2½ cups
1 cup	milk	2 cups
	Salt	
	Black pepper	
	Crushed red pepper (optional)	

Cream of Fennel and Potato Soup

Fresh fennel bulb imparts a light licorice flavor to this Italian-style potato soup.

1. In a large saucepan heat oil over medium heat. Add fennel, yellow onion, and garlic; cook for 5 to 6 minutes or until fennel and onion are tender, stirring occasionally. Add broth, potatoes, milk, and thyme. Bring to boiling; reduce heat. Simmer, covered, for 10 to 15 minutes or until potatoes are tender. Cool slightly.

2. Meanwhile, in a medium nonstick skillet cook sausage over medium heat until browned, using a wooden spoon to break up sausage as it cooks. Drain off fat.

3. Transfer soup, in batches, to a food processor or blender. Cover and process or blend until smooth. Return soup to saucepan. Stir in sausage and lemon juice; heat through.

4. Ladle soup into serving bowls. If desired, sprinkle with green onions.

PER SERVING *254 cal., 9 g fat (2 g sat. fat), 39 mg chol., 831 mg sodium, 29 g carb., 7 g fiber, 17 g pro.*

START TO FINISH 30 minutes

4 servings	ingredients	8 servings
1 Tbsp.	olive oil	2 Tbsp.
3 cups	chopped fennel	6 cups
¾ cup	chopped yellow onion	1½ cups
1 clove	garlic, minced	2 cloves
2½ cups	reduced-sodium chicken broth	5 cups
8 oz.	yellow-flesh potatoes, peeled and sliced	16 oz.
¾ cup	fat-free milk	1½ cups
¼ tsp.	dried thyme, crushed	½ tsp.
8 oz.	uncooked bulk turkey Italian sausage	16 oz.
1½ tsp.	lemon juice	1 Tbsp.
	Slivered green onions (optional)	

Tortilla Soup

Cooked chicken breast is handy to have to add to salads, sandwiches and soups—such as this one. On the weekend, bake a few bone-in breasts, then cool, wrap tightly in plastic wrap, and store in the refrigerator up to 4 days.

1. In a large skillet heat oil over medium heat. Add tortilla strips; cook and stir until crisp. Using a slotted spoon, remove tortilla strips and drain on paper towels.

2. In a large saucepan combine broth and salsa. Bring to boiling over medium-high heat. Stir in chicken and zucchini; heat through.

3. If desired, top each serving with sour cream and/or cilantro. Serve with tortilla strips and, if desired, lime wedges.

PER SERVING *262 cal., 11 g fat (2 g sat. fat), 53 mg chol., 920 mg sodium, 16 g carb., 3 g fiber, 26 g pro.*

START TO FINISH **20 minutes**

4 servings	ingredients	8 servings
2 Tbsp.	vegetable oil	4 Tbsp.
3	6-inch corn tortillas, cut into strips	6
two 14.5-oz. cans	reduced-sodium chicken broth	four 14.5-oz. cans
1 cup	red or green salsa	2 cups
2 cups	cubed cooked chicken	4 cups
1½ cups	coarsely chopped zucchini	3 cups
	Sour cream (optional)	
	Snipped fresh cilantro (optional)	
	Lime wedges (optional)	

Chicken, Brie, and Nectarine Flatbread

The sweetness and acidity of ripe nectarines combines beautifully with rich, buttery Brie on these flatbreads. Serve as a whole meal or cut in small pieces to serve as appetizers.

1. Preheat oven to 425°F. Place flatbreads on a baking sheet. Brush preserves over each flatbread to within ½ inch of edges. Layer chicken, Brie, nectarines, and red onion slices on flatbreads.

2. Bake flatbreads for 10 to 12 minutes or until edges are golden and cheese just begins to melt. Top with greens and drizzle with dressing.

PER SERVING *603 cal., 24 g fat (8 g sat. fat), 108 mg chol., 998 mg sodium, 62 g carb., 5 g fiber, 35 g pro.*

PREP 15 minutes   BAKE 10 minutes at 425°F

4 servings	ingredients	8 servings
4	7-inch flatbreads	8
¼ cup	peach preserves	½ cup
2 cups	shredded purchased roasted chicken	4 cups
4 oz.	Brie, sliced	8 oz.
2	nectarines, pitted and sliced	4
4	thin red onion slices	8
3 cups	arugula, baby lettuce, and/or spinach	6 cups
¼ cup	bottled Italian salad dressing	½ cup

Cucumber-Chicken Pita Sandwiches

These Greek-inspired pitas are terrific picnic food when you store the dressing and assembled sandwiches separately. Right before serving, drizzle each one with dressing.

1. For dressing, in a small bowl combine yogurt, cucumber, dill, and mint.

2. To assemble sandwiches, layer pita bread rounds with lettuce, chicken, tomato, and cheese. Top with dressing. Fold pita bread in half and, if desired, secure with wooden toothpicks.

PER SERVING *290 cal., 5 g fat (2 g sat. fat), 46 mg chol., 503 mg sodium, 37 g carb., 2 g fiber, 23 g pro.*

START TO FINISH **15 minutes**

4 servings	ingredients	8 servings
½ cup	plain low-fat yogurt	1 cup
¼ cup	finely chopped cucumber	½ cup
½ tsp.	dried dill	1 tsp.
¼ tsp.	dried mint, crushed	½ tsp.
4	large pita bread rounds	8
4	lettuce leaves	8
6 oz.	thinly sliced cooked chicken breast	12 oz.
1	small tomato, thinly sliced	2
⅓ cup	crumbled basil-and-tomato-flavor feta cheese	⅔ cup

Indian-Spiced Chicken Pitas

Garam masala is an Indian spice blend that usually contains some combination of pepper, cinnamon, cloves, coriander, cumin, cardamom, dried chiles, fennel, mace, and nutmeg. It adds a sense of warmth—but not heat—to foods.

START TO FINISH 30 minutes

4 servings	ingredients	8 servings
1 cup	plain fat-free yogurt	2 cups
1 tsp.	garam masala	2 tsp.
½ tsp.	bottled hot pepper sauce	1 tsp.
¼ tsp.	salt	½ tsp.
12 oz.	skinless, boneless chicken breast halves, cut into bite-size strips	24 oz.
	Nonstick cooking spray	
2	whole wheat pita bread rounds, halved crosswise	4
1 cup	fresh or refrigerated mango and papaya slices, drained and coarsely chopped	2 cups
1 Tbsp.	snipped fresh mint leaves	2 Tbsp.

1. In a small bowl combine yogurt, garam masala, hot pepper sauce, and salt. Pour three-fourths of the sauce into a resealable plastic bag; refrigerate the remaining sauce until serving time. Add chicken to sauce in plastic bag. Seal bag; turn to coat chicken. Marinate in the refrigerator for 15 minutes. Drain chicken, discarding sauce.

2. Coat an unheated large nonstick skillet with cooking spray. Heat skillet over medium heat. Add chicken to hot skillet; cook for 5 minutes or until tender and no longer pink, turning once.

3. To serve, divide chicken evenly among pita bread halves. Drizzle with the reserved yogurt sauce. Top with chopped fruit; sprinkle with fresh mint.

PER SERVING *249 cal., 2 g fat (0 g sat. fat), 51 mg chol., 430 mg sodium, 32 g carb., 3 g fiber, 26 g pro.*

Turkey and Bean Chili

Chili is always a welcome option for feeding a crowd. Set out a toppings bar of diced onion, sour cream, sliced pickled jalapeños, chopped cilantro, shredded cheese, and hot sauce so each guest can customize his or her bowlful.

1. In a 4- to 6-quart Dutch oven cook ground turkey, celery, carrots, onion, garlic, chili powder, cumin, salt, and black pepper in hot oil over medium heat until turkey is browned and vegetables are tender, using a wooden spoon to break up turkey as it cooks.

2. Stir in tomatoes, green chile peppers (if using), and beans. Bring to boiling; reduce heat. Simmer, covered, for 15 minutes, stirring occasionally. If desired, sprinkle individual servings with cheese.

FOR 8 SERVINGS In Step 1 use a 6- to 8-quart Dutch oven.

PER SERVING *232 cal., 3 g fat (1 g sat. fat), 23 mg chol., 502 mg sodium, 34 g carb., 12 g fiber, 23 g pro.*

PREP 25 minutes   COOK 15 minutes

4 servings	ingredients	8 servings
4 oz.	ground turkey breast	8 oz.
1 stalk	celery, coarsely chopped	2 stalks
1 medium	carrot, coarsely chopped	2 medium
½ medium	onion, coarsely chopped	1 medium
2 cloves	garlic, minced	3 cloves
1 Tbsp.	chili powder	2 Tbsp.
1 tsp.	ground cumin	2 tsp.
¼ tsp.	salt	½ tsp.
¼ tsp.	black pepper	½ tsp.
1½ tsp.	olive oil	1 Tbsp.
three 14.5-oz. cans	no-salt-added fire-roasted diced tomatoes or no-salt-added diced tomatoes, undrained	six 14.5-oz. cans
½ 4-oz. can	diced green chile peppers, undrained (optional)	1 4-oz. can
one 15-oz. can	dark red kidney beans, rinsed and drained	two 15-oz. cans
¼ cup	shredded reduced-fat cheddar cheese (optional)	½ cup

Buffalo-Style Turkey Wraps

When you make the marinade for the turkey tenderloins, mix up the blue cheese dressing and store it in the refrigerator until serving time.

1. Cut each turkey tenderloin in half horizontally to make steaks. Place turkey steaks in a resealable plastic bag set in a shallow dish. For marinade, in a small bowl combine hot pepper sauce, oil, paprika, salt, and cayenne pepper. Pour over turkey in bag; seal bag. Turn to coat turkey. Marinate in the refrigerator for 2 to 3 hours, turning bag occasionally. Drain turkey steaks, discarding marinade.

2. Meanwhile, for the blue cheese dressing, in a blender or food processor combine sour cream, mayonnaise, blue cheese, lemon juice, garlic, and salt. Cover and blend or process until nearly smooth. Cover and chill until serving time.

3. For a gas or charcoal grill, place turkey steaks on the grill rack directly over medium heat. Cover and grill for 12 to 15 minutes or until turkey is done (165°F), turning once halfway through grilling. Wrap tortillas tightly in foil. Place on the grill rack with the turkey; heat for 10 minutes, turning once.

4. Slice turkey. Divide sliced turkey, carrots, celery, and lettuce among the warm tortillas. Top with blue cheese dressing. Roll up tortillas; serve immediately.

PER SERVING *377 cal., 19 g fat (5 g sat. fat), 63 mg chol., 513 mg sodium, 28 g carb., 3 g fiber, 24 g pro.*

PREP 35 minutes   MARINATE 2 hours   GRILL 12 minutes

6 servings	ingredients	12 servings
2 (1 to 1½ lb.)	turkey breast tenderloins	4 (2 to 3 lb.)
3 Tbsp.	bottled hot pepper sauce	6 Tbsp.
2 Tbsp.	vegetable oil	¼ cup
2 tsp.	paprika	4 tsp.
¼ tsp.	salt	½ tsp.
¼ tsp.	cayenne pepper	½ tsp.
½ cup	sour cream	1 cup
¼ cup	mayonnaise	½ cup
¼ cup	crumbled blue cheese	½ cup
1 Tbsp.	fresh lemon juice	2 Tbsp.
1 clove	garlic, sliced	2 cloves
⅛ tsp.	salt	¼ tsp.
six 10-inch	flour tortillas	twelve 10-inch
1½ cups	carrots cut into thin strips	3 cups
1½ cups	thinly bias-sliced celery	3 cups
3 cups	shredded lettuce	6 cups

Tomato-Basil Turkey Burgers

Ground turkey breast ensures that these burgers are lean—but it can easily get overcooked and dry. Be sure to take the burgers off the grill as soon as they reach an internal temperature of 165°F.

1. In a large bowl combine ground turkey, basil, dried tomatoes, salt, and black pepper; mix well. Shape turkey mixture into ½-inch-thick patties.

2. For a gas or charcoal grill, place patties on the grill rack directly over medium heat. Cover and grill for 10 to 13 minutes or until no longer pink (165°F), turning once halfway through grilling and adding cheese for the last 1 to 2 minutes of grilling.

3. Meanwhile, for pesto mayonnaise, in a bowl combine mayonnaise and pesto. Place arugula on bottoms of buns and spread with pesto mayonnaise. Top with burgers and, if desired, roasted pepper strips. Replace tops of buns.

*TIP To roast sweet peppers on the grill, quarter peppers lengthwise; remove stems, seeds, and membranes. For a charcoal or gas grill, place pepper quarters, skin sides down, on grill rack. Cover and grill about 10 minutes or until peppers are charred and very tender. Wrap peppers in foil; let stand about 15 minutes or until cool enough to handle. Peel off and discard skins. Cut peppers into strips.

**TIP If desired, for 4 servings, use ⅓ cup bottled roasted red sweet pepper strips in place of the ½ yellow sweet pepper. For 8 servings, use ¾ cup bottled roasted red sweet pepper strips in place of the 1 yellow sweet pepper.

PER SERVING *328 cal., 5 g fat (2 g sat. fat), 65 mg chol., 700 mg sodium, 33 g carb., 2 g fiber, 35 g pro.*

PREP 20 minutes GRILL 10 minutes

4 servings	ingredients	8 servings
1 lb.	ground turkey breast	2 lb.
1 Tbsp.	snipped fresh basil	2 Tbsp.
1 Tbsp.	finely chopped oil-packed dried tomatoes	2 Tbsp.
½ tsp.	sea salt	1 tsp.
¼ tsp.	freshly ground black pepper	½ tsp.
2 oz.	smoked or fresh mozzarella cheese, thinly sliced	4 oz.
¼ cup	low-fat mayonnaise	½ cup
1 Tbsp.	basil pesto	2 Tbsp.
1 cup	lightly packed arugula or watercress	2 cups
4	sourdough or other hamburger buns, split and toasted	8
½	yellow sweet pepper, roasted* and cut into strips** (optional)	1

Grilled Cherry Tomato Turkey Burgers

Instead of a bun top, these burgers—served on squares of toasted focaccia or ciabatta roll halves—are crowned with juicy grilled cherry tomatoes and fresh basil.

1. In a medium bowl combine half the mustard, the panko, milk, garlic, shallot, basil, half the salt, and half of the pepper. Add ground turkey; mix well. Form into four ½-inch-thick patties.

2. Thread cherry tomatoes on eight skewers (see tip, page 6). Brush lightly with olive oil.

3. For a gas or charcoal grill, place patties on the grill rack directly over medium heat. Cover and grill for 11 to 13 minutes or until patties are done (165°F), turning once halfway through grilling. Add the tomato kabobs the last 6 minutes of grilling, turning to cook evenly.

4. Spread the cut sides of toasted bread with the remaining mustard. Place each burger on top. Remove tomatoes from skewers and pile on the burgers. Drizzle with a little lemon juice and sprinkle with remaining salt and pepper. Top with additional snipped fresh basil.

PER SERVING *297 cal., 7 g fat (1 g sat. fat), 55 mg chol., 821 mg sodium, 24 g carb., 2 g fiber, 33 g pro.*

SOAK 30 minutes   PREP 25 minutes   GRILL 11 minutes

4 servings	ingredients	8 servings
2 Tbsp.	Dijon mustard	¼ cup
2 Tbsp.	whole wheat or plain panko bread crumbs	¼ cup
2 Tbsp.	fat-free milk	¼ cup
2 cloves	garlic, minced	4 cloves
2 Tbsp.	shallot, finely chopped	¼ cup
1 Tbsp.	snipped fresh basil	2 Tbsp.
½ tsp.	salt	1 tsp.
½ tsp.	freshly ground black pepper	1 tsp.
1 lb.	uncooked ground turkey breast	2 lb.
1 pint	cherry tomatoes	2 pints
	Olive oil	
two 4-inch	squares split focaccia bread or ciabatta rolls, toasted	four 4-inch
1 tsp.	lemon juice	2 tsp.
	Snipped fresh basil	

Tex-Mex Turkey Patties

Grilling the onion and sweet pepper in a foil packet intensifies flavor and makes cleanup a snap.

PREP 20 minutes GRILL 10 minutes

2 servings	ingredients	4 servings
8 oz.	uncooked ground turkey breast	1 lb.
¼ cup	salsa	½ cup
¼ tsp.	ground cumin	½ tsp.
⅛ tsp.	black pepper	¼ tsp.
Dash	salt	⅛ tsp.
½ cup	thinly sliced sweet onion (such as Vidalia or Walla Walla)	1 cup
½ cup	red sweet pepper strips	1 cup
1 tsp.	canola oil	2 tsp.
2	tostada shells	4
¼	medium avocado, seeded, peeled, and sliced or chopped	½

1. In a medium bowl combine ground turkey, salsa, cumin, black pepper, and salt; mix well. Shape turkey mixture into ½-inch-thick patties.

2. Fold a 24×12-inch piece of heavy foil in half to make a 12-inch square. Place onion and sweet pepper in the center of foil; drizzle with oil. Bring up two opposite edges of foil; seal with a double fold. Fold the remaining ends to completely enclose vegetables, leaving space for steam to build.*

3. For a gas or charcoal grill, place patties and vegetable packet on the grill rack directly over medium heat. Cover and grill for 10 to 13 minutes or until patties are done (165°F) and vegetables are tender, turning once halfway through grilling.

4. Serve burgers on tostada shells. Top with vegetables and avocado.

*TIP Or, in a skillet cook the onion and sweet pepper in hot oil over medium heat for 10 minutes, stirring occasionally. Cook, uncovered, for 3 minutes more or until pepper is very tender and onion is golden brown, stirring occasionally.

FOR 4 SERVINGS In Step 2 make two vegetable packets.

PER SERVING 285 cal., 10 g fat (1 g sat. fat), 55 mg chol., 430 mg sodium, 20 g carb., 5 g fiber, 29 g pro.

CHAPTER 3

Meat

Whether they're grilled, roasted, stir-fried, or broiled, hearty and flavorful cuts of beef, pork, and lamb satisfy even the biggest appetites.

81

101

104

Steak with Fennel and Beans

Beef shoulder petite tenders are similar in shape to the tenderloin but are less expensive and smaller—hence, the "petite" designation. If you can't find it, use tenderloin instead.

1. In a large skillet heat oil over medium-high heat. Sprinkle beef with salt and pepper then add to the pan. Cook for 24 minutes or until medium rare (145°F), turning once halfway through cooking. Remove steaks; cover with foil. Let stand 10 minutes before slicing.

2. Meanwhile, use a sharp knife to cut off the fennel stalks (about 1 inch above the bulb). Discard stalks, reserving 2 tablespoons of the feathery fronds. Cut a thin slice off the root end of the bulb. Cut bulb into thin wedges. Cut away and discard tough core from each wedge.

3. Add broth to hot skillet. Cook and stir, scraping up browned bits from the bottom of the pan. Add fennel wedges; cook for 4 minutes. Add onion, tomatoes, garlic, and fennel seed; cook about 5 minutes or just until vegetables are tender. Add beans and vinegar; cook for 3 minutes more. Sprinkle with fennel fronds. Serve beans, vegetables, and pan juices with sliced steak.

PER SERVING *350 cal., 13 g fat (4 g sat. fat), 79 mg chol., 473 mg sodium, 26 g carb., 8 g fiber, 37 g pro.*

PREP 15 minutes
COOK 36 minutes

4 servings	ingredients	8 servings
1 Tbsp.	olive oil	2 Tbsp.
two 10-oz.	beef shoulder petite tenders	four 10-oz.
	Salt and black pepper	
1 small	fennel bulb	2 small
½ cup	reduced-sodium beef broth	1 cup
½ cup	chopped onion	1 cup
1 cup	grape tomatoes, halved	2 cups
2 cloves	garlic, minced	4 cloves
1 Tbsp.	fennel seed, coarsely crushed	2 Tbsp.
one 15-oz. can	cannellini beans, rinsed and drained	two 15-oz. cans
2 Tbsp.	balsamic vinegar	¼ cup

Flat-Iron Steak with BBQ Beans

The classic combination of steak and beans is modified for busy cooks. Thanks to canned beans and bottled barbecue sauce, it can be on the table on less than 30 minutes from the time you walk in the door.

1. Trim fat from steaks. Sprinkle steaks with fajita seasoning. Lightly coat a grill pan with cooking spray; preheat grill pan over medium-high heat. Grill steaks for 8 to 12 minutes for medium rare (145°F) or 12 to 15 minutes for medium (160°F), turning once halfway through grilling. On same grill pan, grill tomato slices for 1 to 2 minutes, turning once.

2. Meanwhile, in a medium microwave-safe bowl stir together black beans and barbecue sauce. Cover with vented plastic wrap. Microwave on high for 3 minutes or until heated through, stirring once.

3. Slice steaks and serve with beans and tomatoes. If desired, serve with corn bread and pickled jalapeños.

PER SERVING *272 cal., 8 g fat (2 g sat. fat), 67 mg chol., 667 mg sodium, 25 g carb., 6 g fiber, 29 g pro.*

PREP 15 minutes
GRILL 12 minutes

4 servings	ingredients	8 servings
1½ lb.	boneless beef shoulder top blade (flat iron) steaks	3 lb.
2 tsp.	fajita seasoning	4 tsp.
	Nonstick cooking spray	
2 to 3	medium tomatoes, sliced	4 to 6
one 15-oz. can	black beans, rinsed and drained	two 15-oz. cans
⅓ cup	bottled barbecue sauce	⅔ cup
	Corn bread (optional)	
	Pickled jalapeños (optional)	

Herbed Steaks with Horseradish

Two powerful prepared condiments—Dijon mustard and head-clearing horseradish—give this quick steak dish awesome flavor in a flash.

4 servings	ingredients	8 servings
two 12- to 14-oz.	beef top loin steaks, cut 1 inch thick	four 12- to 14-oz.
	Salt and black pepper	
2 Tbsp.	prepared horseradish	¼ cup
1 Tbsp.	Dijon mustard	2 Tbsp.
2 tsp.	snipped fresh flat-leaf parsley	4 tsp.
1 tsp.	snipped fresh thyme	2 tsp.
1 recipe	Broiled Cherry Tomatoes and Sweet Peppers (optional)	2 recipes

1. Preheat broiler. Trim fat from steaks. Lightly sprinkle steaks with salt and pepper. Place steaks on the unheated rack of broiler pan. Broil 4 to 5 inches from heat for 7 minutes.

2. Meanwhile, in a small bowl stir together horseradish, mustard, parsley, and thyme.

3. Turn steaks. Broil for 8 to 9 minutes more for medium (160°F). The last 1 minute of broiling, spread horseradish mixture over steaks. If desired, serve with Broiled Cherry Tomatoes and Sweet Peppers.

PER SERVING *284 cal., 15 g fat (6 g sat. fat), 84 mg chol., 351 mg sodium, 1 g carb., 0 g fiber, 33 g pro.*

*BROILED CHERRY TOMATOES AND SWEET PEPPERS
In a medium bowl place 1 yellow and/or red sweet pepper cut into strips and 1 cup cherry tomatoes. Drizzle with 2 tablespoons olive oil and ¼ teaspoon each salt and black pepper. Add to the broiler pan in Step 3 after turning the steaks.

Flat-Iron Steak with Avocado Butter

Rich, fruity avocado is blended with butter, lime juice, herbs, and a spike of cayenne to make an indulgent-tasting topping for tender grilled steaks.

1. For the Avocado Butter, in a medium bowl combine avocado, butter, lime juice, parsley, tarragon, salt, and, if desired, cayenne pepper. Using a fork, gently mash the ingredients together until thoroughly combined but still somewhat chunky. Spoon Avocado Butter into a small bowl; chill until almost firm.

2. Trim fat from steaks. Brush steaks with olive oil. For rub, in a small bowl combine herbes de Provence, salt, and pepper. Sprinkle evenly over both sides of steaks; rub in with your fingers. If desired, cover and chill steaks up to 24 hours.

3. For a charcoal grill, grill steaks on the rack of an uncovered grill directly over medium coals to desired doneness, turning once halfway through grilling. Allow 7 to 9 minutes for medium rare (145°F) and 10 to 12 minutes for medium (160°F). (For a gas grill, preheat grill. Reduce heat to medium. Place steaks on the grill rack over heat. Cover and grill as directed.) Serve Avocado Butter with steaks.

PER SERVING *369 cal., 25 g fat (10 g sat. fat), 109 mg chol., 463 mg sodium, 3 g carb., 2 g fiber, 33 g pro.*

PREP 20 minutes
GRILL 7 minutes

6 servings	ingredients	12 servings
1	ripe avocado, halved, seeded, peeled, and chopped	2
¼ cup	butter, softened	½ cup
3 Tbsp.	fresh lime juice	6 Tbsp.
2 Tbsp.	snipped fresh flat-leaf parsley	¼ cup
1 Tbsp.	snipped fresh tarragon	2 Tbsp.
¼ tsp.	salt	½ tsp.
⅛ tsp.	cayenne pepper (optional)	¼ tsp.
6	beef shoulder top blade (flat-iron) steaks or boneless ribeye steaks, cut ¾ inch thick	12
1 Tbsp.	olive oil	2 Tbsp.
1 Tbsp.	herbes de Provence, crushed	2 Tbsp.
½ tsp.	salt	1 tsp.
½ tsp.	freshly ground black pepper	1 tsp.

Pan-Fried Garlic Steak with White Beans

Ribeye steaks are often sold in 12-ounce or 8-ounce portions. If you can't find 4- to 5-ounce steaks, cut the larger steaks into smaller portions before grilling.

1. Lightly drizzle steaks with olive oil; sprinkle with salt and pepper.

2. Heat an extra-large skillet over medium-high heat. Add steaks; reduce heat to medium. Cook for 6 to 8 minutes or until desired doneness (145°F for medium rare), turning once. Remove steaks from skillet; cover and keep warm. Add garlic to skillet. Cook and stir for 1 minute or until softened; remove garlic from skillet.

3. Add beans and butter to skillet; heat through. Add parsley; cook for 1 minute more. Top steaks with garlic and serve with beans.

PER SERVING *326 cal., 18 g fat (7 g sat. fat), 81 mg chol., 425 mg sodium, 16 g carb., 5 g fiber, 29 g pro.*

START TO FINISH 30 minutes

4 servings	ingredients	8 servings
four 4- to 5-oz.	beef ribeye steaks (Delmonico)	eight 4- to 5-oz.
	Olive oil	
	Salt and black pepper	
6 cloves	garlic, peeled and thinly sliced	12 cloves
one 15- to 19-oz. can	cannellini (white kidney) beans	two 15- to 19-oz. cans
2 Tbsp.	butter	¼ cup
¼ cup	snipped fresh flat-leaf parsley	½ cup

Quick Skillet Steaks with Mushrooms

Serve these mushroom-topped steaks with mashed potatoes and snow peas that have been briefly stir-fried in a little sesame oil and a sprinkling of salt.

1. Trim fat from steaks. Sprinkle steaks with pepper and salt. Heat a large skillet over medium-high heat. Add oil; swirl to lightly coat skillet. Reduce heat to medium. Add steaks; cook for 8 to 10 minutes or until medium rare (145°F), turning once. Transfer steaks to a tray or plate; cover with foil and keep warm while preparing sauce.

2. For sauce, in the same skillet cook mushrooms and onions over medium-high heat about 5 minutes or until tender, stirring frequently. Add garlic; cook and stir for 1 minute more. Carefully add wine. Boil gently, uncovered, for 5 minutes, stirring occasionally. In a small bowl combine broth and flour; stir into mushroom mixture. Cook and stir until thickened and bubbly. Cook and stir for 1 minute more.

3. Cut steaks in half and return to skillet; heat through, turning to coat steaks with sauce. Transfer steaks and sauce to dinner plates. Garnish with parsley.

PER SERVING *287 cal., 11 g fat (4 g sat. fat), 64 mg chol., 330 mg sodium, 11 g carb., 2 g fiber, 28 g pro.*

START TO FINISH 30 minutes

4 servings	ingredients	8 servings
two 8-oz.	boneless beef top loin steaks, cut ¾ to 1 inch thick	four 8-oz.
½ tsp.	cracked black pepper	1 tsp.
¼ tsp.	salt	½ tsp.
1 tsp.	olive oil	2 tsp.
8 oz.	fresh mushrooms, quartered	16 oz.
1 cup	frozen small whole onions	2 cups
4 cloves	garlic, minced	8 cloves
¾ cup	dry red wine	1½ cups
1 cup	50% less sodium beef broth	2 cups
2 Tbsp.	whole wheat flour	¼ cup
	Fresh flat-leaf parsley	

Grilled Steak Bruschetta Salad

This delicious jumble of grilled steak, greens, tangly blue cheese, and crunchy toasted bread is a bit like a deconstructed sandwich.

START TO FINISH 30 minutes

4 servings	ingredients	8 servings
⅓ cup	apricot preserves	⅔ cup
¼ cup	plain low-fat yogurt	½ cup
2 Tbsp.	creamy Dijon mustard blend or honey mustard	¼ cup
2 Tbsp.	lemon juice	¼ cup
two 8- to 10-oz.	boneless beef top loin (strip) steaks, cut 1 inch thick	four 8- to 10-oz.
¼ tsp.	salt	½ tsp.
¼ tsp.	black pepper	½ tsp.
12	¼-inch slices baguette-style French bread	24
4 cups	fresh spinach	8 cups
¼ cup	chopped roasted red sweet pepper	½ cup
¼ cup (1 oz.)	crumbled Gorgonzola cheese or shredded Parmesan cheese	½ cup (2 oz.)

1. For dressing, snip any large pieces of fruit in preserves. In a small bowl combine preserves, yogurt, mustard blend, and lemon juice. Set aside.

2. Trim fat from steaks. Sprinkle both sides of steaks with salt and black pepper.

3. For a gas or charcoal grill, place steaks on the grill rack directly over medium heat. Cover and grill for 10 to 12 minutes for medium-rare (145°F) or 12 to 15 minutes for medium (160°F), turning once halfway through grilling. Add bread slices to grill the last 1 to 2 minutes of grilling. Cover and grill until bread is toasted, turning once.

4. Divide spinach among dinner plates. Top with toasted bread slices; drizzle with dressing. Slice steaks; arrange on bread slices. Top with roasted pepper and cheese.

PER SERVING *404 cal., 16 g fat (7 g sat. fat), 55 mg chol., 621 mg sodium, 39 g carb., 2 g fiber, 24 g pro.*

Beef and Noodle Salad

The ribbons of cucumber in this Asian-style salad are made with a regular vegetable peeler.

1. Preheat broiler. In a small bowl combine soy sauce and the 1 tablespoon chili sauce; brush evenly over both sides of the steak. Place on the unheated rack of a broiler pan. Broil 4 to 5 inches from heat for 15 to 18 minutes or until desired doneness (160°F for medium), turning once halfway through broiling. Thinly slice beef across the grain.

2. Meanwhile, cook noodles according to package directions; drain in a colander set in sink. Rinse with cold water.

3. Slice cucumber crosswise into thirds. Using a vegetable peeler, cut lengthwise ribbons from each third.

4. Stir together the ½ cup chili sauce and the water. Divide steak, noodles, cucumber, and carrots among bowls. Drizzle with chili sauce mixture; top with cilantro.

FOR 8 SERVINGS In Step 1 use 2 tablespoons Asian sweet chili sauce, and in Step 4, use 1 cup chili sauce.

PER SERVING *492 cal., 9 g fat (4 g sat. fat), 76 mg chol., 999 mg sodium, 71 g carb., 2 g fiber, 27 g pro.*

START TO FINISH **30 minutes**

4 servings	ingredients	8 servings
1 Tbsp.	soy sauce	2 Tbsp.
1 Tbsp.	Asian sweet chili sauce	2 Tbsp.
1 lb.	beef flank steak, trimmed of fat	2 lb.
8 oz.	rice noodles	1 lb.
1	medium English cucumber	2
½ cup	Asian sweet chili sauce	1 cup
½ cup	water	1 cup
1 cup	purchased fresh julienned carrots	2 cups
	Fresh cilantro	

Caprese Pasta and Steak

Add steak and pesto-dressed pasta to a classic caprese salad of fresh mozzarella, tomatoes, and basil and you have a one-dish meal.

START TO FINISH 30 minutes

4 servings	ingredients	8 servings
8 oz.	dried large rigatoni pasta	1 lb.
½ cup	purchased basil pesto	1 cup
1 lb. cut into 4 portions	boneless beef shoulder top blade (flat-iron) or tri-tip steak	2 lb. cut into 8 portions
4 oz.	fresh mozzarella cheese, sliced	8 oz.
4	roma tomatoes, sliced	8
	Fresh basil leaves (optional)	

1. Cook pasta according to package directions; drain. Return to hot pan.

2. Meanwhile, brush one-fourth of the pesto onto steaks. Heat a large heavy skillet over medium heat; add steaks. Cook for 10 minutes or until desired doneness, turning once.

3. Add the remaining pesto to pasta in pan; toss to coat. Divide pasta among dinner plates. Top with steaks, cheese, and tomato slices. If desired, top with fresh basil.

PER SERVING *695 cal., 35 g fat (6 g sat. fat), 94 mg chol., 486 mg sodium, 53 g carb., 3 g fiber, 40 g pro.*

Chili-Cheese Hoagies

A bolillo is a crusty Mexican sandwich roll, similar to a small hoagie with the texture of French bread. You can find them in Mexican grocery stores. If they are unavailable in your area, substitute French bread rolls.

1. Preheat oven to 375°F. In a large skillet cook ground beef, onion, sweet peppers, and garlic over medium-high heat until meat is browned and vegetables are tender, using a wooden spoon to break up meat as it cooks. Drain off fat.

2. Stir in tomatoes and black pepper. Bring to boiling; reduce heat. Simmer, uncovered, for 15 minutes or until mixture is thickened, stirring occasionally.

3. Spoon some of the filling onto each bolillo; top with cheese. Place filled bolillos on a baking sheet. Bake for 5 minutes or until bread is lightly toasted and cheese is melted.

PER SERVING *738 cal., 31 g fat (15 g sat. fat), 91 mg chol., 1,274 mg sodium, 79 g carb., 5 g fiber, 36 g pro.*

PREP 25 minutes
COOK 15 minutes
BAKE 5 minutes at 375°F

6 servings	ingredients	12 servings
1 lb.	lean ground beef	2 lb.
1 cup	chopped onion	2 cups
1 cup	chopped green sweet peppers	2 cups
2 cloves	garlic, minced	4 cloves
one 14.5-oz. can	diced tomatoes with chili spices, undrained	two 14.5-oz. cans
¼ tsp.	black pepper	½ tsp.
6	bolillos, split	12
1 cup (4 oz.)	shredded Monterey Jack cheese	2 cups (8 oz.)
1 cup (4 oz.)	shredded cheddar cheese	2 cups (8 oz.)

Spicy Apricot Lamb Chops

There are two types of lamb chops—rib chops and loin chops. Rib chops—featured in this recipe—are cut from the rib rack. They have a small slender bone attached to a tender scallop of meat. Loin chops have a "T-bone" in the center and are thicker and meatier.

PREP 20 minutes
BROIL 8 minutes

4 servings	ingredients	8 servings
8	lamb rib chops, cut ¾ to 1 inch thick	16
1 Tbsp.	packed brown sugar	2 Tbsp.
1 tsp.	garlic salt	2 tsp.
1 tsp.	chili powder	2 tsp.
1 tsp.	paprika	2 tsp.
½ tsp.	dried oregano, crushed	1 tsp.
¼ tsp.	ground cinnamon	½ tsp.
¼ tsp.	ground allspice	½ tsp.
¼ tsp.	black pepper	½ tsp.
¼ cup	apricot preserves	½ cup

1. Preheat broiler. Trim fat from chops. In a small bowl combine brown sugar, garlic salt, chili powder, paprika, oregano, cinnamon, allspice, and black pepper. Sprinkle spice mixture on all sides of the chops; rub in with your fingers.

2. Place chops on the unheated rack of a broiler pan. Broil 4 to 5 inches from the heat for 8 to 12 minutes for medium (145°F), turning chops and brushing with preserves once halfway through broiling.

PER SERVING *311 cal., 8 g fat (3 g sat. fat), 119 mg chol., 345 mg sodium, 18 g carb., 1 g fiber, 39 g pro.*

Mediterranean Lamb Skillet

This elegant dish is ideal for weeknight entertaining. It goes together in less than 30 minutes yet is special enough for company.

1. Cook orzo according to package directions; drain and keep warm. Meanwhile, trim fat from chops. Sprinkle with salt and pepper. In a large skillet heat olive oil over medium heat. Add chops; cook in hot oil for 9 to 11 minutes for medium (160°F), turning once halfway through cooking. Remove chops from skillet; keep warm.

2. Stir garlic into drippings in skillet. Cook and stir for 1 minute. Stir in tomatoes, vinegar, and the snipped rosemary. Bring to boiling; reduce heat. Simmer, uncovered, for 5 minutes. Stir in orzo and olives. Spoon onto four dinner plates; arrange two chops on each plate. Sprinkle with pine nuts and, if desired, top with rosemary sprigs.

PER SERVING *678 cal., 51 g fat (20 g sat. fat), 105 mg chol., 886 mg sodium, 28 g carb., 2 g fiber, 27 g pro.*

START TO FINISH 25 minutes

4 servings	ingredients	8 servings
½ cup	dried orzo	1 cup
8	lamb rib chops, cut 1 inch thick	16
	Salt and black pepper	
1 tsp.	olive oil	2 tsp.
3 cloves	garlic, minced	6 cloves
one 14.5-oz. can	diced tomatoes with basil, garlic, and oregano, undrained	two 14.5-oz. cans
1 Tbsp.	balsamic vinegar	2 Tbsp.
2 tsp.	snipped fresh rosemary	4 tsp.
⅓ cup	halved, pitted kalamata olives	⅔ cup
2 Tbsp.	pine nuts, toasted (see tip, page 24)	¼ cup
	Fresh rosemary sprigs (optional)	

Grilled Pork and Pineapple

Pineapple is custom-built for the grill. The sturdy, sweet slices hold up beautifully to the heat and the flavor of the fruit is only improved with a touch of smoke and light charring.

1. Cut pineapple into ½-inch slices; set aside. Trim fat from pork chops. Sprinkle chops lightly with salt and pepper to taste.

2. For a charcoal or gas grill, place chops on the grill rack directly over medium heat. Cover and grill for 3 minutes. Turn chops and add pineapple to grill rack. Brush chops and pineapple with 2 tablespoons of the marmalade. Cover and grill for 2 to 4 minutes more or until an instant-read thermometer inserted into pork registers 145°F, turning pineapple halfway through grilling. Remove chops and pineapple from grill; let chops rest at least 3 minutes.

3. Meanwhile, in a small bowl combine Greek yogurt and the remaining marmalade. Arrange pineapple and chops on plates. Sprinkle with fresh thyme; serve with yogurt sauce.

FOR 8 SERVINGS In Step 2 brush chops and pineapple with 4 tablespoons of the marmalade.

PER SERVING *301 cal., 6 g fat (3 g sat. fat), 97 mg chol., 220 mg sodium, 27 g carb., 2 g fiber, 35 g pro.*

PREP 15 minutes
GRILL 5 minutes

4 servings	ingredients	8 servings
1	fresh pineapple, peeled and cored	2
4	boneless top loin pork chops, cut ¾ inch thick	8
	Salt and black pepper	
3 Tbsp.	orange marmalade	6 Tbsp.
½ cup	plain Greek yogurt	1 cup
2 tsp.	snipped fresh thyme	4 tsp.

Crispy Baked Pork Chops and Potatoes

If you have a small crowd coming for dinner and not much time to get food ready, this pork chop-and-potato combo will save the day. If you don't say a word, no one will be the wiser that it relies on a couple of convenience products. While it bakes, toss together a big green salad.

PREP 10 minutes
BAKE 15 minutes at 425°F

4 servings	ingredients	8 servings
1	egg	2
2 Tbsp.	milk	¼ cup
1 cup	corn bread stuffing mix, crushed	2 cups
four (1 to 1½ lb. total)	pork loin chops, cut ½ inch thick	eight (2 to 3 lb. total)
	Salt and black pepper	
one 20-oz. pkg.	frozen roasted tri-cut potatoes	two 20-oz. pkg.

1. Preheat oven to 425°F. In a shallow dish beat egg with a fork; stir in milk. Place dry stuffing mix in another shallow dish. Trim fat from chops. Season chops with salt and pepper. Dip pork chops into egg mixture. Coat both sides with stuffing mix. Arrange pork chops in a single layer in one side of a 15×10×1-inch baking pan. Add potatoes to the opposite side of the same pan, mounding potatoes as needed to fit.

2. Bake, uncovered, for 15 to 20 minutes or until pork is done (145°F) and potatoes are lightly browned and crisp, turning pork and stirring potatoes once.

PER SERVING *442 cal., 18 g fat (4 g sat. fat), 92 mg chol., 1,407 mg sodium, 51 g carb., 2 g fiber, 18 g pro.*

Smoked Pork Chops with Mustard-Dill Sauce

Smoked pork chops give this super-quick dish a jump-start on flavor. Classic mustard-dill sauce takes it over the top.

1. Preheat broiler. Place chops on the unheated rack of a broiler pan. Broil 3 to 4 inches from the heat for 9 to 12 minutes or until heated through, turning once halfway through broiling.

2. Meanwhile, for sauce, in a small bowl stir together brown sugar and vinegar until sugar is dissolved. Using a wire whisk, beat in mustard, olive oil, dill, and pepper until well combined. Transfer warm chops to a serving platter. Drizzle smoked chops with some of the sauce. Pass remaining sauce.

PER SERVING *208 cal., 11 g fat (2 g sat. fat), 45 mg chol., 1,453 mg sodium, 7 g carb., 0 g fiber, 15 g pro.*

PREP 10 minutes
BROIL 9 minutes

6 servings	ingredients	12 servings
6	smoked pork loin chops, cut 1 inch thick	12
3 Tbsp.	packed brown sugar	6 Tbsp.
3 Tbsp.	cider vinegar or white wine vinegar	6 Tbsp.
½ cup	Dijon mustard	1 cup
3 Tbsp.	olive oil	6 Tbsp.
½ tsp.	dried dill	1 tsp.
⅛ tsp.	black pepper	¼ tsp.

Southwest Pork Chops

A can of Mexican-style beans, a can of corn, and your favorite salsa give Southwest-style flavor to this speedy dish.

1. Trim fat from chops. Coat an extra-large nonstick skillet with cooking spray. Heat skillet over medium-high heat. Add chops, half at a time if necessary, to hot skillet; cook about 4 minutes or until browned, turning once halfway through cooking. Remove chops from skillet.

2. Add chili beans, salsa, and corn to skillet; stir to combine. Place chops on top of bean mixture. Bring to boiling; reduce heat. Simmer, covered, for 12 to 18 minutes or until chops are slightly pink in centers and juices run clear (145°F). Serve over hot cooked rice. If desired, sprinkle with cilantro.

PER SERVING *379 cal., 10 g fat (3 g sat. fat), 71 mg chol., 490 mg sodium, 38 g carb., 5 g fiber, 33 g pro.*

START TO FINISH **30 minutes**

6 servings	ingredients	12 servings
6 (about 2½ lb. total)	bone-in pork rib chops, cut ¾ inch thick	12 (about 5 lb. total)
	Nonstick cooking spray	
one 15-oz. can	Mexican-style or Tex-Mex-style chili beans	two 15-oz. cans
1 cup	salsa	2 cups
1 cup	frozen whole kernel corn	2 cups
3 cups	hot cooked rice	6 cups
	Snipped fresh cilantro (optional)	

Pork Loin with Parsnips and Pears

Root vegetables have garnered new appreciation during the last few years. Creative cooks have figured out interesting ways to prepare them—boiled and mashed, pan-fried, grated into hash, stirred into stews, or roasted. Parsnips, which look like large white carrots, have a natural sweetness that is intensified when cooked.

1. Slice pork ½ inch thick; sprinkle lightly with salt and pepper. Brush with some of the Pickapeppa sauce.

2. In an extra-large skillet heat oil over medium heat; add pork and brown on each side. Transfer pork to a plate; cover and keep warm. In the same skillet cook parsnips and pears, stirring occasionally, for 5 minutes or until parsnips are crisp-tender. Stir remaining Pickapeppa sauce and pear nectar into skillet. Return pork to skillet. Cook for 3 minutes more or just until a trace of pink remains in pork. Transfer pork and vegetables to a serving platter. Continue to boil sauce, uncovered, until slightly thickened.

3. Pour sauce over pork, pears , and parsnips to serve. If desired, sprinkle with parsley.

PER SERVING *399 cal., 15 g fat (4 g sat. fat), 94 mg chol., 318 mg sodium, 28 g carb., 4 g fiber, 38 g pro.*

START TO FINISH 25 minutes

4 servings	ingredients	8 servings
1½ lb.	boneless pork loin	3 lb.
	Salt and black pepper	
3 Tbsp.	Pickapeppa or Worcestershire sauce	6 Tbsp.
1 Tbsp.	olive oil	2 Tbsp.
3 to 4	small parsnips, peeled and sliced	6 to 8
2	pears, cored and sliced or chopped	4
½ cup	pear nectar or apple juice	1 cup
	Fresh flat-leaf parsley (optional)	

Jamaican Pork Stir-Fry

4 servings	ingredients	8 servings
1 Tbsp.	vegetable oil	2 Tbsp.
one 14.4-oz. pkg.	frozen stir-fry vegetables (green, red, and yellow sweet peppers and onion)	two 14.4-oz. pkg.
12 oz.	pork strips for stir-frying	24 oz.
2 to 3 tsp.	Jamaican jerk seasoning	4 to 6 tsp.
½ cup	bottled plum sauce	1 cup
1 Tbsp.	soy sauce (optional)	2 Tbsp.
	Chopped peanuts (optional)	
2 cups	hot cooked rice or pasta	4 cups

If you can't find precut pork strips for stir-frying, cut your own from boneless pork loin.

1. In a large skillet or wok heat oil over medium-high heat. (Add more oil as necessary during cooking.) Add frozen vegetables; cook and stir for 5 to 7 minutes or until vegetables are crisp-tender. Drain any excess liquid from the skillet. Remove vegetables from skillet.

2. Toss meat with jerk seasoning; add to hot skillet. Cook and stir for 2 to 4 minutes or until meat is slightly pink in center.

3. Add plum sauce to meat in skillet; return vegetables to skillet. Gently stir all ingredients together to coat with sauce; heat through. If desired, season with soy sauce and sprinkle with peanuts. Serve stir-fry over hot cooked rice.

PER SERVING *336 cal., 6 g fat (1 g sat. fat), 54 mg chol., 421 mg sodium, 45 g carb., 2 g fiber, 22 g pro.*

Italian Pork with Sweet Potatoes

The number of servings you need—4 or 8—will determine which size slow cooker to use. If you do a lot of slow cooking, it's a good idea to have two sizes of cookers—a 3½- to 4-quart and a 5- to 6-quart.

1. Trim fat from meat. If necessary, cut meat to fit into a 3½- or 4-quart slow cooker. For rub, in a small bowl combine fennel seeds, garlic powder, oregano, paprika, salt, and pepper. Sprinkle rub evenly over meat; rub in with your fingers.

2. Place sweet potatoes in the prepared slow cooker; top with meat. Pour broth over potatoes and meat. Cover and cook on low-heat setting for 8 to 10 hours or on high-heat setting for 4 to 5 hours.

3. Remove meat from cooker, reserving cooking liquid. Shred or slice meat. Using a slotted spoon, remove sweet potatoes from cooking liquid. Serve meat and sweet potatoes with the cooking liquid. If desired, sprinkle with parsley.

FOR 8 SERVINGS In Step 1 use a 5- to 6-quart slow cooker.

PER SERVING *341 cal., 10 g fat (4 g sat. fat), 110 mg chol., 490 mg sodium, 24 g carb., 4 g fiber, 36 g pro.*

PREP **20 minutes**
SLOW COOK **8 hours (low) or 4 hours(high)**

4 servings	ingredients	8 servings
1½- to 2-lb.	boneless pork shoulder roast	3- to 4-lb.
1 tsp.	fennel seeds, crushed	2 tsp.
½ tsp.	garlic powder	1 tsp.
½ tsp.	dried oregano, crushed	1 tsp.
½ tsp.	paprika	1 tsp.
¼ tsp.	salt	½ tsp.
¼ tsp.	black pepper	½ tsp.
1 lb.	sweet potatoes, peeled and cut into 1-inch pieces	2 lb.
1 cup	reduced-sodium chicken broth	2 cups
	Fresh flat-leaf parsley, sliced (optional)	

Maple-Pork Wilted Salad

Pork has a natural sweetness that invites glazing with maple syrup, brown sugar, jelly, or jam—or pairing it with fruit such as apples, pears, plums, or peaches.

1. In a large bowl combine spinach, cucumber, onion, and almonds; set aside. Trim fat from meat. Cut meat into ¼-inch slices. Sprinkle with salt and pepper.

2. In a large skillet heat 1 tablespoon of the oil over medium-high heat. Add meat; cook for 2 to 3 minutes or just until meat is slightly pink in center, turning once. Add meat to bowl with spinach mixture; set aside.

3. For dressing, in the same skillet heat the remaining oil over medium heat. Add shallot; cook and stir for 2 minutes or until tender. Add vinegar and maple syrup. Simmer, uncovered, for 2 minutes or until slightly thickened. Season to taste with additional salt and pepper.

4. Pour dressing over salad; toss gently to coat. Top each serving with cheese.

FOR 8 SERVINGS In Step 2 use an extra-large skillet and heat 2 tablespoons of the oil.

PER SERVING 325 cal., 15 g fat (4 g sat. fat), 67 mg chol., 349 mg sodium, 23 g carb., 3 g fiber, 24 g pro.

START TO FINISH 30 minutes

4 servings	ingredients	8 servings
8 cups	fresh baby spinach or torn fresh spinach	16 cups
1 (about 1½ cups)	medium cucumber, peeled, seeded, and chopped	2 (about 3 cups)
⅓ cup	thin red onion wedges	⅔ cup
¼ cup	sliced almonds, toasted (see tip, page 24)	½ cup
12 oz.	pork tenderloin	1½ lb.
¼ tsp.	salt	½ tsp.
¼ tsp.	black pepper	½ tsp.
2 Tbsp.	olive oil	¼ cup
2 Tbsp.	finely chopped shallot	¼ cup
¼ cup	cider vinegar	½ cup
¼ cup	pure maple syrup	½ cup
	Salt and black pepper	
⅓ cup	shredded smoked Gouda or cheddar cheese	⅔ cup

Roasted BLT Salad

The best BLT requires perfectly ripe tomatoes. This salad, inspired by that favorite summer sandwich, calls for cherry tomatoes, so it can be made any time of year.

1. Preheat oven to 400°F. In a large skillet cook bacon until crisp; drain on paper towels. Break into large pieces; set aside.

2. Meanwhile, line a 15×10×1-inch baking pan with foil. Add cherry tomatoes; toss with 2 teaspoons of the olive oil. Bake, uncovered, for 10 minutes. Transfer tomatoes and their juices to a medium bowl. Place bread cubes and romaine quarters on the baking pan. Drizzle romaine with 2 teaspoons of the olive oil. Return pan to oven; bake for 5 minutes or until bread is golden and romaine is browned on edges.

3. Add bread to the medium bowl with the tomatoes. Toss gently to combine. Let stand for 5 minutes to allow bread to absorb some of the tomato juices. Transfer tomatoes, bread, romaine, and bacon to a serving platter. Drizzle with remaining olive oil. Sprinkle with salt and pepper.

FOR 8 SERVINGS In Step 2 line two 15×10×1-inch baking pans with foil. Toss cherry tomatoes with 4 teaspoons of the olive oil. Drizzle romaine with 4 teaspoons olive oil.

PER SERVING *258 cal., 10 g fat (2 g sat. fat), 9 mg chol., 647 mg sodium, 31 g carb., 2 g fiber, 8 g pro.*

PREP **15 minutes**
BAKE **15 minutes at 400°F**
STAND **5 minutes**

4 servings	ingredients	8 servings
4 slices	bacon	8 slices
1 cup	cherry tomatoes	2 cups
6 tsp.	olive oil	12 tsp.
½	baguette, cut into 1½-inch cubes	1
1 head	romaine lettuce, quartered lengthwise	2 heads
¼ tsp.	salt	½ tsp.
¼ tsp.	black pepper	½ tsp.

Brats with Mango Relish

Most mangoes in the produce section of the supermarket are not ready to eat. If they are hard, take them home and let them ripen on the counter for a few days. A perfectly ripe mango will yield slightly to pressure and will be fragrant.

1. Lightly brush mango and onion with vegetable oil.

2. For a charcoal or gas grill, place mango halves, onion slices, and brats on the grill rack directly over medium heat. Cover and grill for 8 minutes or until mango and brats are browned and heated through and onion is crisp-tender, turning once halfway through grilling. Set aside mango, onion, and brats. Lightly brush romaine with vegetable oil. Grill romaine for 1 to 2 minutes or until lightly browned and wilted, turning once. Lightly toast buns for 1 to 2 minutes on grill.

3. For mango relish, chop grilled mango and onion. In a medium bowl combine mango, onion, the 1 tablespoon oil, and the jerk seasoning. Season to taste with salt and pepper. Serve brats in buns with relish and romaine on the side.

FOR 8 SERVINGS In Step 3 use 2 tablespoons oil.

PER SERVING *478 cal., 31 g fat (6 g sat. fat), 66 mg chol., 1,112 mg sodium, 35 g carb., 2 g fiber, 15 g pro.*

START TO FINISH 20 minutes

4 servings	ingredients	8 servings
1	large fresh mango, halved, seeded, and peeled	2
1	small red onion, cut into ½-inch slices	2
	Vegetable oil	
4 (12 oz. total)	cooked smoked bratwurst	8 (24 oz. total)
2	hearts of romaine lettuce, halved	4
4	hoagie buns, brat buns, or other crusty rolls, split	8
1 Tbsp.	vegetable oil	2 Tbsp.
½ tsp.	Jamaican jerk seasoning	1 tsp.
	Salt and black pepper	

Gorgonzola-Sauced Tortellini with Artichokes

4 servings	ingredients	8 servings
one 9-oz. pkg.	refrigerated spinach-cheese tortellini or three-cheese tortellini	two 9-oz. pkg.
8 oz.	bulk sweet or hot Italian sausage	1 lb.
1½ cups (6 oz.)	sliced cremini, stemmed shiitake, or button mushrooms	3 cups (12 oz.)
1	small onion, cut into thin wedges	2
½ cup (2 oz.)	crumbled Gorgonzola cheese	1 cup (4 oz.)
one 14.5-oz. can	diced tomatoes with basil, garlic, and oregano, drained	two 14.5-oz. cans
one 6-oz. jar	marinated artichoke hearts, drained and quartered	two 6-oz. jars
1 Tbsp.	Parmesan cheese shards	2 Tbsp.
2 Tbsp.	small fresh basil leaves	¼ cup

To shave Parmesan, run a vegetable peeler along the wide side of a wedge of the cheese.

1. In a large saucepan cook tortellini according to package directions; drain.

2. Meanwhile, in a large saucepan cook sausage, mushrooms, and onion until sausage is no longer pink and onion is tender, breaking up sausage with a wooden spoon. Drain off fat.

3. Add Gorgonzola cheese to sausage mixture in saucepan; cook and stir over low heat until cheese is melted. Gently stir in tortellini, tomatoes, and artichokes; heat through. Top with Parmesan cheese and basil.

PER SERVING *464 cal., 24 g fat (11 g sat. fat), 71 mg chol., 1,384 mg sodium, 37 g carb., 3 g fiber, 23 g pro.*

Kielbasa and Orzo

This simple, tasty skillet dish is cooked in stages all in one pan—first the sausage, then pasta, then zucchini.

1. In a large skillet heat oil over medium-high heat. Add kielbasa; cook about 2 minutes or until browned. Stir in orzo. Cook and stir for 1 minute.

2. Stir in broth, the water, and Italian seasoning. Bring to boiling; reduce heat. Simmer, covered, about 10 minutes or until orzo is tender, adding the zucchini for the last 5 minutes of cooking and stirring occasionally. If desired, top with green onions. Season to taste with salt and black pepper.

PER SERVING *394 cal., 19 g fat (6 g sat. fat), 60 mg chol., 1,346 mg sodium, 38 g carb., 2 g fiber, 18 g pro.*

START TO FINISH 25 minutes

4 servings	ingredients	8 servings
1 Tbsp.	vegetable oil	2 Tbsp.
12 oz.	cooked kielbasa, halved lengthwise and cut into 1-inch pieces	24 oz.
1 cup	dried orzo	2 cups
one 14.5-oz. can	50%-less-sodium beef broth	two 14.5-oz. cans
½ cup	water	1 cup
1 tsp.	dried Italian seasoning, crushed	2 tsp.
2½ cups	coarsely chopped zucchini	5 cups
⅓ cup	sliced green onions and/or chopped red sweet pepper (optional)	⅔ cup
	Salt and black pepper	

Spicy Sausage Soup with Parmesan Cheese Crisps

Earthy Swiss chard adds flavor, color, and loads of nutrients to this Italian-style soup.

1. If desired, for the Parmesan Cheese Crisps, preheat oven to 400°F. Coarsely shred Parmesan cheese. Line a baking sheet with parchment paper or nonstick foil. For each crisp, place about 1 tablespoon shredded cheese on prepared sheet; pat into a 2-inch circle, allowing 2 inches between circles. Bake for 7 to 8 minutes or until bubbly and lightly golden. Let stand on baking sheet for 1 to 2 minutes or until cooled but still pliable. Carefully peel off paper or foil. Place cheese crisps on a wire rack; cool completely.

2. In a 4-quart Dutch oven cook sausage, onion, and garlic over medium-high heat until meat is browned, using a wooden spoon to break up meat as it cooks. Drain off fat.

3. Add broth and Italian seasoning to sausage. Bring to boiling; reduce heat. Stir in Swiss chard; cook just until wilted. Stir in tomato; cook for 1 minute more. Ladle soup into bowls. If desired, serve with Parmesan Cheese Crisps.

PER SERVING *374 cal., 31 g fat (10 g sat. fat), 88 mg chol., 1,928 mg sodium, 5 g carb., 1 g fiber, 19 g pro.*

START TO FINISH **25 minutes**

4 servings	ingredients	8 servings
6 oz.	Parmesan cheese (optional)	12 oz.
1 lb.	bulk hot or mild pork sausage	2 lb.
¼ cup	chopped onion	½ cup
2 cloves	garlic, minced	4 cloves
one 48-oz. carton	chicken broth	two 48-oz. cartons
½ tsp.	dried Italian seasoning, crushed	1 tsp.
4 cups	coarsely chopped Swiss chard leaves	8 cups
⅓ cup	chopped roma tomato	⅔ cup

Smoked Gouda and Apricot Melts

Chewy bits of dried apricot and almonds give texture to this fancy grilled ham and cheese.

1. In a small bowl combine dried apricots and enough boiling water to cover. Let stand for 5 minutes; drain. Stir almonds and green onions into drained apricots.

2. Spread half the bread slices with apricot preserves. Top with ham. Top with the apricot mixture and cheese; sprinkle with pepper. Add the remaining half bread slices. Lightly coat outsides of sandwiches with cooking spray.

3. Preheat a large nonstick skillet over medium heat. Place sandwiches, half at a time if necessary, in skillet. Weight sandwiches with a heavy skillet and cook for 1 to 2 minutes or until bread is toasted. Turn sandwiches, weight again, and cook for 1 to 2 minutes more or until bread is toasted and filling is heated through.

PER SERVING *419 cal., 14 g fat (6 g sat. fat), 48 mg chol., 863 mg sodium, 55 g carb., 5 g fiber, 20 g pro.*

START TO FINISH 25 minutes

4 servings	ingredients	8 servings
½ cup	dried apricots, snipped	1 cup
	Boiling water	
⅓ cup	sliced, slivered, or chopped almonds, toasted (see tip, page 24)	⅔ cup
¼ cup	thinly sliced green onions	½ cup
8 slices	marbled rye or hearty whole grain bread	16 slices
2 Tbsp.	apricot preserves	¼ cup
4 oz.	thinly sliced cooked ham	8 oz.
1 cup (4 oz.)	shredded smoked Gouda cheese	2 cups (8 oz.)
¼ tsp.	black pepper	½ tsp.
	Nonstick cooking spray	

CHAPTER 4

Seafood

Fish and shellfish are quick-cooking, and most varieties can be conveniently kept on hand in the freezer for fast, flavorful meals any day of the week.

116

122

130

Red Snapper with Herb-Pecan Crust

Pecans, bread crumbs, lemon peel, herbs, and garlic make a richly flavored topping that turns toasty when the fish is grilled.

PREP 15 minutes
GRILL 4 minutes

4 servings	ingredients	8 servings
four 5- to 6-oz.	fresh or frozen red snapper fillets, ½ to 1 inch thick	eight 5- to 6-oz.
⅓ cup	finely chopped pecans	⅔ cup
2 Tbsp.	fine dry bread crumbs	¼ cup
2 Tbsp.	butter, softened	¼ cup
1 tsp.	finely shredded lemon peel	2 tsp.
1 Tbsp.	snipped fresh flat-leaf parsley	2 Tbsp.
¼ tsp.	salt	½ tsp.
⅛ tsp.	black pepper	¼ tsp.
	Dash cayenne pepper	
2 cloves	garlic, minced	4 cloves
	Snipped fresh flat-leaf parsley (optional)	
	Lemon wedges (optional)	

1. Thaw fish, if frozen. Rinse fish; pat dry with paper towels. Measure thickness of fish; set aside. In a small bowl combine pecans, bread crumbs, butter, lemon peel, the 1 tablespoon parsley, the salt, black pepper, cayenne pepper, and garlic. Set aside.

2. For a gas or charcoal grill, place fish, skin sides down, on greased grill rack directly over medium heat. Spoon the pecan topping on fillets; spread slightly. Cover and grill for 4 to 6 minutes per ½-inch thickness of fish or until fish begins to flake when tested with a fork. If desired, sprinkle fish with additional parsley and serve with lemon wedges.

FOR 8 SERVINGS In Step 1 use 2 tablespoons parsley.

PER SERVING *268 cal., 14 g fat (4 g sat. fat), 67 mg chol., 287 mg sodium, 7 g carb., 8 g fiber, 30 g pro.*

Catfish and Slaw Tacos

Crispy Cajun-style catfish fillets star in these tasty tacos. To save time in making the slaw, use preshredded cabbage.

1. Thaw fish, if frozen. Rinse fish; pat dry with paper towels. Cut fish into 1-inch strips; set fish aside.

2. For slaw, in a medium bowl combine mayonnaise, lime juice, and hot pepper sauce. Add cabbage; toss to coat. Set slaw aside.

3. Toss fish strips with Cajun seasoning. In a large bowl combine cornmeal and flour. Add fish; toss to coat.

4. In a large skillet heat oil over medium heat. Cook fish strips, half at a time, in hot oil for 4 to 6 minutes or until golden and fish flakes easily when tested with a fork, turning to brown evenly. Remove from skillet.

5. Wrap tortillas in paper towels. Microwave on high for 1 minute (or toast in a dry skillet). If using corn tortillas, stack two for each taco, or use one flour tortilla for each taco. Divide fish and slaw among tortillas. Reserve any dressing left in bowl to serve with tacos. Serve tacos immediately with reserved dressing, lime wedges, and additional hot pepper sauce.

* Or for 4 servings, use eight 8-inch flour tortillas, and for 8 servings use sixteen 8-inch flour tortillas.

PER SERVING *620 cal., 36 g fat (5 g sat. fat), 59 mg chol., 300 mg sodium, 53 g carb., 3 g fiber, 24 g pro.*

START TO FINISH **30 minutes**

4 servings	ingredients	8 servings
1 lb.	fresh or frozen catfish fillets	2 lb.
¼ cup	mayonnaise	½ cup
3 Tbsp.	lime juice	6 Tbsp.
½ tsp.	bottled hot pepper sauce	1 tsp.
2½ cups	shredded cabbage	5 cups
1 Tbsp.	Cajun seasoning	2 Tbsp.
¼ cup	cornmeal	½ cup
¼ cup	all-purpose flour	½ cup
¼ cup	vegetable oil (more as needed)	½ cup
sixteen 4-inch	corn tortillas*	thirty-two 4-inch
	Lime wedges	
	Bottled hot pepper sauce	

Fish Tacos with Chipotle Cream

Freeze leftover chipotle peppers for future use. Divide the peppers and sauce into small portions and freeze in small freezer bags or tightly sealed plastic containers.

1. Thaw fish, if frozen. Rinse fish; pat dry with paper towels. Brush oil evenly on both sides of fish. For rub, in a small bowl stir together chili powder, cumin, salt, and black pepper. Sprinkle rub over both sides of fish; rub in with your fingers.

2. For chipotle cream, in another small bowl stir together sour cream and chopped chipotle pepper; set aside. Wrap tortillas tightly in foil.

3. For a gas or charcoal grill, place fish and tortilla packet on the greased grill rack directly over medium heat. Cover and grill for 4 to 6 minutes or until fish begins to flake when tested with a fork and tortillas are heated through, turning fish and tortilla packet once halfway through grilling.

4. Using a fork, break fish into pieces. Fill warm tortillas evenly with cabbage, fish, and avocado slices. Serve with, chipotle cream, fresh salsa, lime wedges, and, if desired, cilantro.

PER SERVING *293 cal., 9 g fat (3 g sat. fat), 35 mg chol., 493 mg sodium, 34 g carb., 4 g fiber, 19 g pro.*

FISH TOSTADAS Prepare as above, except for 6 servings substitute 6 tostada shells for the tortillas; for 12 servings substitute 12 tostada shells. Do not grill tostada shells. Top shells with cabbage, fish, avocado, chipotle cream, salsa, lime wedges, and, if desired, cilantro.

PREP 25 minutes
GRILL 4 minutes

6 servings	ingredients	12 servings
four 4-oz.	fresh or frozen skinless red snapper, tilapia, or sole fillets, ½ inch thick	eight 4-oz.
1 Tbsp.	cooking oil	2 Tbsp.
1 tsp.	ancho chili powder	2 tsp.
½ tsp.	ground cumin	1 tsp.
¼ tsp.	salt	½ tsp.
¼ tsp.	black pepper	½ tsp.
½ cup	sour cream	1 cup
1 tsp.	finely chopped canned chipotle pepper in adobo sauce	2 tsp.
twelve 6-inch	corn or flour tortillas	twenty-four 6-inch
2 cups	shredded cabbage or romaine lettuce	4 cups
1	ripe avocado, halved, seeded, peeled, and cut into thin slices (optional)	2
1 cup	refrigerated fresh salsa	2 cups
1	lime, cut into wedges	2
	Snipped cilantro (optional)	

Herb-Crusted Cod with Cauliflower Mash

Cod has a rich, buttery texture and mild flavor that lends itself to all sorts of flavors and preparations. Sometimes simple is best—such as these crispy herbed fillets.

1. Place vegetables in a Dutch oven. Add ½ teaspoon of the salt and enough water to cover. Cover and bring to boiling. Reduce heat to medium. Cook, covered, for 15 to 20 minutes or until tender. Drain vegetables, reserving some of the cooking water. Using a potato masher, mash potatoes to desired consistency, adding reserved water as needed. Stir in cheese. Season to taste with salt and pepper. Cover and keep warm.

2. Meanwhile, preheat oven to 300°F. Rinse fish and pat dry with paper towels. Cut into 8 equal pieces. In a shallow dish beat egg. In another shallow dish combine bread crumbs, dill, remaining salt, and ½ teaspoon pepper. Dip fish pieces into egg, then into bread crumb mixture. Set aside.

3. In a large skillet heat olive oil over medium-high heat. Add half the fish. Cook for 2 to 3 minutes on each side or until fish is golden brown and flakes easily with a fork. Drain on paper towels. Keep warm while frying remaining fish. Serve with cauliflower mash and lemon wedges. If desired, sprinkle with additional fresh herbs.

FOR 8 SERVINGS In Step 1 add 1 teaspoon of the salt to the water. In Step 2 cut fish into 16 equal pieces, and use 1 teaspoon black pepper

PER SERVING *317 cal., 12 g fat (5 g sat. fat), 122 mg chol., 778 mg sodium, 21 g carb., 3 g fiber, 31 g pro.*

START TO FINISH **30 minutes**

4 servings	ingredients	8 servings
4½ cups	cauliflower florets, baby gold potatoes, and/or peeled carrots, coarsely chopped	9 cups
1 tsp.	salt	2 tsp.
2 oz.	semisoft cheese with garlic and fine herbs	4 oz.
	Black pepper	
4 (about 1¼ lb.)	fresh cod fillets	8 (about 2½ lb.
1	egg	2
⅔ cup	panko bread crumbs	1⅓ cups
2 Tbsp.	snipped fresh dill	¼ cup
½ tsp.	black pepper	1 tsp.
1 Tbsp.	olive oil	2 Tbsp.
	Lemon wedges	
	Fresh herbs (optional)	

Grilled Cod with Red Pepper Sauce

Red sweet peppers, tomatoes, vinegar, and a hint of cayenne are blended to make a fresh and vibrant sauce for this simple grilled fish.

PREP 30 minutes
GRILL 4 minutes

4 servings	ingredients	8 servings
four to six 4-oz.	fresh or frozen skinless cod fillets	ten to twelve 4-oz.
1¼ cups (1 large)	chopped red sweet pepper	2½ cups (2 large)
2 Tbsp.	olive oil	4 Tbsp.
1 cup (2 medium)	peeled, seeded, and chopped tomatoes	2 cups (4 medium)
2 Tbsp.	white wine vinegar	¼ cup
¼ tsp.	salt	½ tsp.
Dash	cayenne pepper	⅛ tsp.
1 Tbsp.	snipped fresh* basil or oregano	2 Tbsp
	Red and/or yellow cherry tomatoes (optional)	
	Fresh basil or oregano sprigs (optional)	

1. Thaw fish, if frozen. Rinse fish; pat dry with paper towels. Measure thickness of fish; set aside.

2. For sauce, in a small skillet heat half the oil. Cook sweet pepper in hot oil over medium heat for 3 to 5 minutes or until tender, stirring occasionally. Stir in chopped tomatoes, half the vinegar, the salt, and cayenne pepper. Cook for 5 minutes or until tomatoes are softened, stirring occasionally. Cool slightly. Transfer to a blender or food processor. Cover and blend until smooth. Return sauce to skillet; cover and keep warm.

3. In a small bowl stir together the remaining vinegar, remaining oil, and snipped fresh or dried basil; brush over both sides of fish. Place fish in a greased grill basket, tucking under any thin edges.

4. For a gas or charcoal grill, place grill basket on the grill rack directly over medium heat. Cover and grill for 4 to 6 minutes per ½-inch thickness of fish or until fish begins to flake when tested with a fork, turning basket once halfway through grilling.

5. Serve fish with sauce. If desired, garnish with cherry tomatoes and fresh basil sprigs.

*TIP If desired, for 4 servings use 1 teaspoon dried basil or oregano, crushed, for the 1 tablespoon fresh snipped basil or oregano. For 8 servings use 2 teaspoons dried basil or oregano, crushed, for the 2 tablespoons fresh snipped basil or oregano.

PER SERVING *194 cal., 8 g fat (1 g sat. fat), 41 mg chol., 223 mg sodium, 4 g carb., 1 g fiber, 26 g pro.*

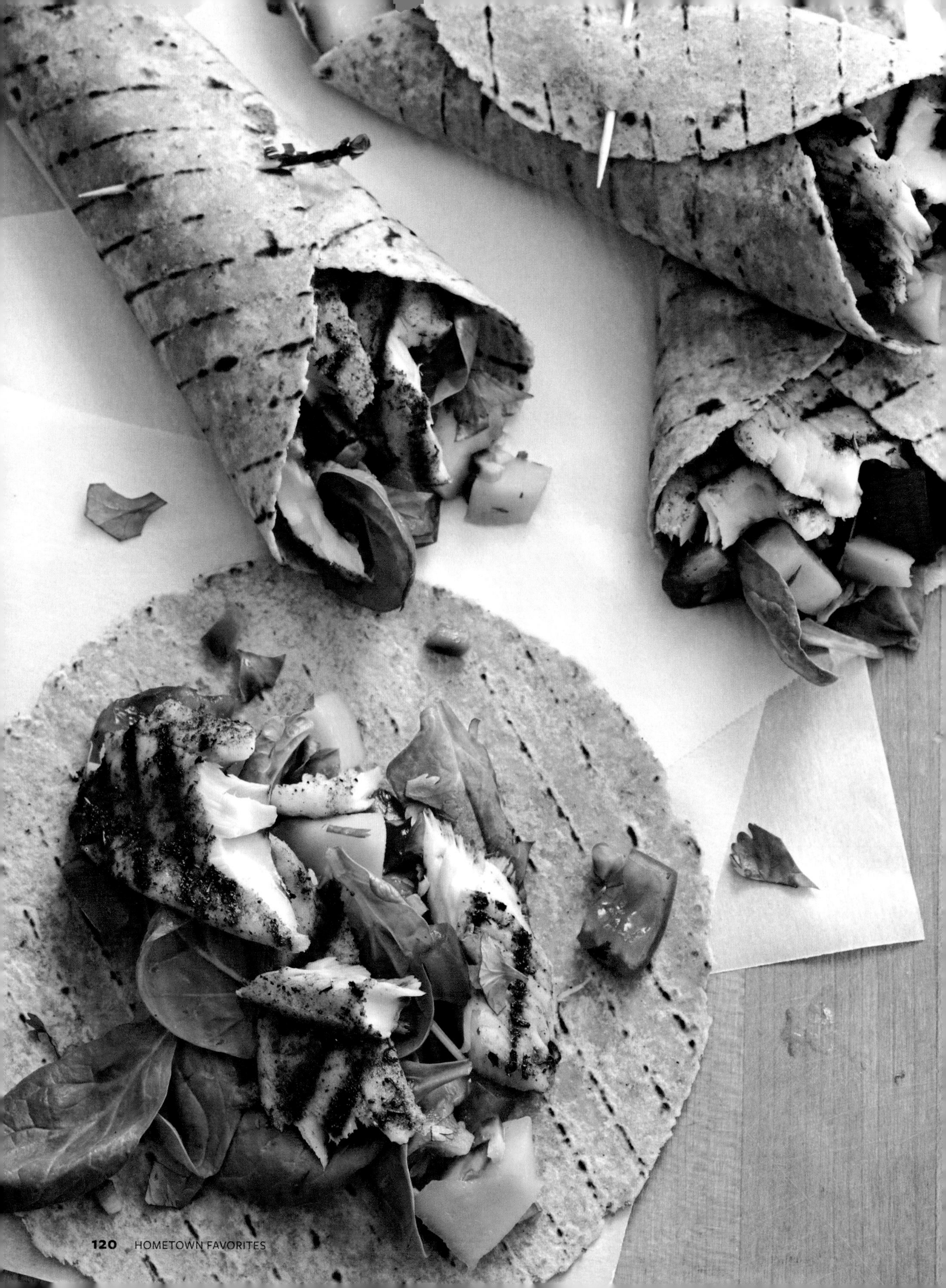

Grilled Jamaican Jerk Fish Wraps

Apply the grilling time in this flavorful recipe—4 to 6 minutes per ½-inch thickness—to almost any fish recipe.

1. Thaw fish, if frozen. In a medium bowl toss together spinach, tomato, mango, cilantro, jalapeño, and lime juice; set aside.

2. Rinse fish; pat dry with paper towels. Sprinkle jerk seasoning evenly over both sides of fish; rub in with your fingers. Measure thickness of fish.

3. For a charcoal or gas grill, place tortillas on the greased grill rack directly over medium heat. Cover and grill for 2 minutes or until tortillas have grill marks, turning once halfway through grilling. Remove from grill. Place fish on grill rack. Cover and grill for 4 to 6 minutes per ½-inch thickness or until fish flakes easily when tested with a fork, turning once halfway through grilling. Remove fish from grill. Coarsely flake fish with a fork.

4. To serve, place tortillas, grill mark sides down, on a work surface. Divide spinach mixture and flaked fish among tortillas. Roll up each tortilla and cut in half.

PER SERVING *254 cal., 4 g fat (1 g sat. fat), 48 mg chol., 509 mg sodium, 23 g carb., 11 g fiber, 29 g pro.*

PREP 30 minutes
GRILL 4 minutes

4 servings	ingredients	8 servings
1 lb.	fresh or frozen skinless flounder, cod, or sole fillets	2 lb.
2 cups	packaged fresh baby spinach	4 cups
¾ cup	seeded and chopped tomato	1½ cups
¾ cup	chopped fresh mango or pineapple	1½ cups
2 Tbsp.	snipped fresh cilantro	¼ cup
1 Tbsp.	seeded and finely chopped fresh jalapeño (see tip, page 19)	2 Tbsp.
1 Tbsp.	lime juice	2 Tbsp.
1½ tsp.	Jamaican jerk seasoning	1 Tbsp.
four 7- to 8-inch	whole grain flour tortillas	eight 7- to 8-inch

Creamy Tuna-Noodle Toss

When you crave low-stress comfort food, this is it. It's a terrific meal from the pantry and freezer. Nearly all of the ingredients are staples you likely have on hand at any given moment.

4 servings	ingredients	8 servings
6 oz.	wide egg noodles	12 oz.
1½ cups	frozen peas	3 cups
3 Tbsp.	butter	6 Tbsp.
1	small red onion, quartered and sliced	2
2 cloves	garlic, minced	4 cloves
¼ tsp.	black pepper	½ tsp.
2 Tbsp.	all-purpose flour	¼ cup
1¼ cups	milk	2½ cups
one 5-oz. can	solid white tuna, drained and broken into chunks	two 5-oz. cans
½ cup	grated Parmesan cheese	1 cup
	Milk	
	Salt	
1 Tbsp.	fresh lemon juice	2 Tbsp.
	Black pepper	

1. Cook noodles according to package directions, adding the peas for the last 2 minutes of cooking time. Drain and return to pan.

2. Meanwhile, in a medium saucepan melt butter. Add onion, garlic, and the ¼ teaspoon black pepper; cook and stir over medium heat about 3 minutes or just until onion is tender. Stir in flour until blended. Add the 1¼ cups milk all at once. Cook and stir until thickened and bubbly. Remove from heat; add tuna and cheese.

3. Pour tuna mixture over noodles and peas in pan. Toss gently to combine. If desired, stir in additional milk, 1 tablespoon at a time, until sauce reaches desired consistency. Season to taste with salt. Divide among four shallow bowls. Drizzle with lemon juice. Sprinkle with additional pepper.

FOR 8 SERVINGS In Step 2 use ½ teaspoon black pepper and 2½ cups milk.

PER SERVING *438 cal., 16 g fat (9 g sat. fat), 89 mg chol., 614 mg sodium, 48 g carb., 4 g fiber, 25 g pro.*

Thai Tuna Kabobs

Pick your pepper based on how much heat you like in your food. Thai chiles are the hottest of the options in this recipe, serranos are in the middle, and jalapeños are the mildest.

PREP 30 minutes
MARINATE 2 hours
GRILL 10 minutes

4 servings	ingredients	8 servings
1 lb.	fresh or frozen tuna steaks, cut 1 inch thick	2 lb.
¼ cup	snipped fresh cilantro	½ cup
1 tsp.	finely shredded lemon peel or lime peel	2 tsp.
3 Tbsp.	lemon juice or lime juice	6 Tbsp.
3 Tbsp.	rice vinegar	6 Tbsp.
1 to 2	fresh Thai, serrano, or jalapeño chile peppers, seeded and finely chopped (see tip, page 19)	2 to 4
1 tsp.	sesame seeds	2 tsp.
1 tsp.	toasted sesame oil	2 tsp.
2	medium zucchini, cut into 1-inch slices	4
1	medium red onion, cut into 8 wedges	2
	Lime wedges (optional)	

1. Thaw fish, if frozen. Rinse fish; pat dry with paper towels. Cut fish into 1-inch pieces; set aside. For marinade, in a small bowl combine half the cilantro, the lemon peel, lemon juice, vinegar, chile pepper, sesame seeds, and oil; set aside.

2. On eight skewers (see tip, page 6), alternately thread fish,* zucchini, and red onion, leaving ¼ inch between pieces. Place kabobs on a platter or in a shallow dish. Brush ¼ cup of the marinade over kabobs. Cover and marinate in the refrigerator for 2 to 4 hours. Cover and chill the remaining marinade.

3. For a gas or charcoal grill, place kabobs on the greased grill rack directly over medium heat. Cover and grill for 10 to 12 minutes or until fish begins to flake when tested with a fork but is still slightly pink inside, turning once halfway through grilling.

4. Transfer kabobs to a serving platter. Sprinkle with the remaining cilantro. Serve the remaining chilled marinade as a sauce. If desired, garnish with lime wedges.

*TIP Thread tuna onto skewers perpendicular to the grain of the fish.

FOR 8 SERVINGS In Step 2 brush ½ cup of the marinade over the kabobs.

PER SERVING *215 cal., 7 g fat (2 g sat. fat), 43 mg chol., 58 mg sodium, 8 g carb., 2 g fiber, 28 g pro.*

Citrus Salsa Salmon

This is a lovely recipe to make during winter, when oranges and grapefruit are at peak season.

1. Preheat broiler. Rinse salmon with cold water; pat dry with paper towels. Sprinkle salmon with salt and pepper. In a small saucepan melt jelly over low heat. Brush half the melted jelly over the salmon. Set aside remaining jelly.

2. Place salmon on the unheated rack of a broiler pan. Broil 4 inches from the heat for 8 to 10 minutes or until fish flakes easily when tested with a fork.

3. Meanwhile, for fresh citrus salsa, in a medium bowl combine chopped oranges, grapefruit sections, tomatoes, and the remaining melted jelly. Season to taste with additional salt and pepper. Serve with salmon. If desired, serve with salad greens.

PER SERVING *357 cal., 15 g fat (3 g sat. fat), 62 mg chol., 221 mg sodium, 31 g carb., 3 g fiber, 25 g pro.*

PREP 20 minutes
BROIL 8 minutes

4 servings	ingredients	8 servings
four 4- to 5-oz.	skinless salmon fillets, ¾ to 1 inch thick	eight 4- to 5-oz.
¼ tsp.	salt	½ tsp.
⅛ tsp.	black pepper	¼ tsp.
¼ cup	red jalapeño jelly	½ cup
2 medium	oranges, peeled, seeded, and coarsely chopped	4 medium
1 medium	grapefruit, peeled and sectioned	2 medium
1 cup	grape or cherry tomatoes, halved	2 cups
	Salt and black pepper	
	Salad greens (optional)	

Curried Salmon with Tomatoes and Dried Plums

Israeli couscous (also called pearl couscous) is deliciously chewy and fun to eat. Look for it at specialty stores or Middle Eastern food markets if you can't find it at regular supermarket.

1. Thaw fish if frozen. Rinse and pat dry; set aside. Preheat oven to 350°F.

2. In a large ovenproof skillet cook and stir sweet pepper, red onion, celery, and garlic in hot oil over medium-high heat for 3 minutes. Add tomatoes, dried plums, and curry powder. Cook and stir for 2 minutes; remove from heat.

3. Add salmon to skillet; transfer to oven. Bake, uncovered, for 10 minutes or until salmon just begins to flake when tested with a fork.

4. Meanwhile, in a small saucepan, for 4 servings bring 1⅓ cups water to boiling (for 8 servings use 2⅔ cups water). Stir in couscous; return to boiling. Reduce heat. Simmer, covered, about 12 minutes. Remove from heat; cover and let stand for 2 minutes. Drain if necessary.

5. To serve, spoon salmon over couscous. Sprinkle with fresh mint.

PER SERVING *392 cal., 11 g fat (2 g sat. fat), 62 mg chol., 491 mg sodium, 45 g carb., 6 g fiber, 28 g pro.*

PREP 20 minutes
COOK 20 minutes
BAKE 10 minutes at 350°F

4 servings	ingredients	8 servings
1 lb.	fresh or frozen skinless salmon fillet, cut into 1½-inch cubes	2 lb.
1	medium green sweet pepper, chopped	2
½ cup	chopped red onion	1 cup
1	stalk celery, chopped	2
2 cloves	garlic, minced	4 cloves
1 Tbsp.	olive oil	2 Tbsp.
two 14.5-oz. cans	diced tomatoes, undrained	four 14.5-oz. cans
½ cup	dried plums, coarsely chopped	1 cup
2 tsp.	curry powder	4 tsp.
⅔ cup	Israeli couscous, regular couscous, rice, or orzo	1⅓ cups
	Fresh mint leaves	

Seared Scallops with Ginger Sauce

To get the best sear on the scallops, be sure they are nice and dry before cooking.

1. Thaw scallops, if frozen. Rinse scallops; pat dry with paper towels. In a large skillet melt butter over medium-high heat. Add scallops to skillet. Cook for 2 to 3 minutes or until scallops are opaque, stirring frequently. Remove scallops from skillet; keep warm.

2. For sauce, add broth, juice concentrate, and ginger to hot skillet. Bring to boiling. Boil, uncovered, until sauce is reduced by about half. Spoon sauce over scallops.

PER SERVING *168 cal., 5 g fat (3 g sat. fat), 48 mg chol., 262 mg sodium, 11 g carb., 0 g fiber, 19 g pro.*

START TO FINISH **15 minutes**

4 servings	ingredients	8 servings
1 lb.	fresh or frozen sea scallops	2 lb.
4 tsp.	butter	3 Tbsp.
⅓ cup	chicken broth	⅔ cup
¼ cup	frozen pineapple-orange juice concentrate, thawed	½ cup
1 tsp.	grated fresh ginger	2 tsp.

Spanish Shrimp Stir-Fry

Buying shrimp that has already been deveined saves prep time. You can choose to leave the tail on for an attractive presentation or cut it off for easier eating.

1. Thaw shrimp, if frozen. Rinse shrimp; pat dry with paper towels. Set aside.

2. In a large skillet or wok heat oil over medium-high heat. Add potatoes; stir to coat with oil. Cook for 3 to 4 minutes or until browned, stirring frequently. Carefully add broth. Cook, covered, for 8 to 10 minutes or until potatoes are tender.

3. Add shrimp to potatoes in skillet. Cook and stir for 3 to 4 minutes or until shrimp are opaque. Stir in salsa, olives, and paprika; heat through. Serve stir-fry over hot cooked rice and, if desired, sprinkle with parsley.

PER SERVING *429 cal., 11 g fat (1 g sat. fat), 138 mg chol., 744 mg sodium, 58 g carb., 3 g fiber, 23 g pro.*

START TO FINISH **35 minutes**

4 servings	ingredients	8 servings
12 oz.	fresh or frozen peeled and deveined medium shrimp	24 oz.
2 Tbsp.	vegetable or canola oil	¼ cup
8 oz.	small red or fingerling potatoes, cut into bite-size chunks	16 oz.
½ cup	chicken broth	1 cup
1 cup	chunky salsa	2 cups
4 oz.	black olives, pitted and sliced	8 oz.
½ tsp.	smoked paprika or chili powder	1 tsp.
4 cups	hot cooked rice or couscous	8 cups
	Snipped fresh flat-leaf parsley (optional)	

Crab Cakes with Apricot Sauce

There are several types of canned crabmeat, including lump, backfin, and claw meat. The best type for crab cakes is backfin. It's not as expensive as lump crabmeat but a little more expensive than claw meat. Backfin meat has enough texture to be appealing when combined with the other ingredients in crab cakes.

PREP 20 minutes
COOK 6 minutes
BAKE 10 minutes at 350°F

4 servings	ingredients	8 servings
2	eggs, lightly beaten	4
1½ cups	panko bread crumbs	3 cups
¼ cup	sliced green onions	½ cup
2 Tbsp.	mayonnaise	¼ cup
2 tsp.	Worcestershire sauce	4 tsp.
	Hot pepper sauce	
two 6-oz. cans	cooked crabmeat, drained, flaked, and cartilage removed	four 6-oz. cans
2 Tbsp.	olive oil	¼ cup
1 Tbsp.	butter	2 Tbsp.
⅓ cup	apricot fruit spread	⅔ cup
1 tsp.	Chinese-style hot mustard	2 tsp.
¼ tsp.	ground ginger	½ tsp.
	Sliced heirloom tomatoes (optional)	
	Fresh dill (optional)	

1. Preheat oven to 350°F. For crab cakes, in a large bowl combine eggs, 1 cup of the panko, the green onions, mayonnaise, Worcestershire, and hot pepper sauce to taste. Fold in crabmeat. Shape into four cakes about 1¼ inches thick. Place remaining panko in a shallow bowl. Add crab cakes; lightly coat both sides.

2. In an extra-large nonstick oven-safe skillet, heat oil and butter over medium-high heat. Add crab cakes. Cook for 6 to 8 minutes or until golden on both sides, turning once. Place skillet in oven and bake for 10 to 15 minutes or until 160°F on an instant-read thermometer.

3. Meanwhile, for Apricot Sauce, in a small microwave-safe bowl stir together apricot fruit spread, mustard, and ginger. Microwave on high for 20 to 30 seconds or until heated through.

4. Spoon Apricot Sauce over crab cakes. Serve with sliced tomatoes and sprinkle with fresh dill, if desired.

FOR 8 SERVINGS In Step 1 use 2 cups of the panko and shape eight cakes about 1¼ inches thick.

PER SERVING *383 cal., 19 g fat (4 g sat. fat), 148 mg chol., 1126 mg sodium, 29 g carb., 1 g fiber, 22 g pro.*

Caribbean Clam Chowder

Classic Caribbean ingredients—sweet potatoes, thyme, lime, and rum—give this island-inspired clam chowder authentic flavor.

1. Chop fresh clams (if using), reserving juice; set clams aside. Strain clam juice to remove bits of shell. (Or drain canned clams, reserving juice.) Add enough water to the reserved clam juice to equal 2½ cups total liquid.

2. In a large saucepan bring the clam liquid to boiling. Stir in sweet potatoes, onion, celery, sweet pepper, dried thyme (if using), and garlic. Return to boiling; reduce heat. Simmer, covered, about 10 minutes or until sweet potatoes are tender.

3. Mash vegetables slightly with a potato masher. Stir in clams, fresh thyme (if using), tomatoes, lime juice, and, if desired, rum. Return to boiling; reduce heat. Simmer, uncovered, for 1 to 2 minutes more.

*TIP If desired, for 4 servings, use ½ teaspoon dried thyme in place of the 1½ teaspoons snipped fresh thyme. For 8 servings, use 1 teaspoon dried thyme in place of the 1 tablespoon snipped fresh thyme.

FOR 8 SERVINGS In Step 1 add water to reserved clam juice to equal 5 cups.

PER SERVING 128 cal., 1 g fat (0 g sat. fat), 19 mg chol., 337 mg sodium, 22 g carb., 3 g fiber, 9 g pro.

START TO FINISH **35 minutes**

4 servings	ingredients	8 servings
½ pint or one 6.5-oz. can	shucked clams or, undrained canned minced clams	1 pint or two 6.5-oz. cans
2 cups	peeled and cubed sweet potatoes	4 cups
½ cup	chopped onion	1 cup
½ cup	chopped celery	1 cup
¼ cup	chopped red sweet pepper	½ cup
1½ tsp.	snipped fresh thyme*	1 Tbsp.
2 cloves	garlic, minced	4 cloves
one 10-oz. can	diced tomatoes and green chiles, undrained	two 10-oz. cans
1 Tbsp.	lime juice	2 Tbsp.
1 Tbsp.	dark rum (optional)	2 Tbsp.

CHAPTER 5

Sides

The entrée may get the most attention, but it's the side dishes—salads, veggie dishes and breads—that round out a meal and make it memorable.

135

149

155

Beets and Greens Dinner Salad

This is a lovely salad to serve with a pork roast for a fall dinner. For a colorful presentation, use both golden and red beets

1. Place whole beets in a microwave-safe casserole; add vinegar, sugar, and the water. Microwave, covered, on high for 9 to 12 minutes or until beets are tender, stirring once. Remove beets, reserving liquid in casserole. Trim stems and slip off skins. Slice beets; set aside.

2. For dressing, whisk oil, salt, and pepper into the reserved cooking liquid. In a large bowl toss together beets, salad greens, and dried cranberries. Pour dressing over greens; toss gently to coat. If desired, sprinkle with pumpkin seeds and cheese.

PER SERVING *232 cal., 14 g fat (2 g sat. fat), 0 mg chol., 371 mg sodium, 26 g carb., 4 g fiber, 3 g pro.*

START TO FINISH **30 minutes**

4 servings	ingredients	8 servings
6	whole mall golden and/or red beets, tops trimmed	12
½ cup	cider vinegar	1 cup
2 Tbsp.	sugar	¼ cup
2 Tbsp.	water	¼ cup
¼ cup	olive oil	½ cup
½ tsp.	salt	1 tsp.
½ tsp.	black pepper	1 tsp.
8 cups	mixed salad greens	16 cups
⅓ cup	dried cranberries	⅔ cup
	Roasted pumpkin seeds (pepitas) (optional)	
	Crumbled goat cheese (chèvre) (optional)	

Citrus Salad

Bibb lettuce—also called Boston or butter lettuce—has a mild flavor and tender texture that blends beautifully with sweet-tart citrus.

1. For dressing, squeeze juice from one orange and transfer to a small bowl. Whisk in oil, tarragon, and mustard.

2. Peel and thinly slice the remaining oranges.

3. Place lettuce in a large bowl. Drizzle with dressing; toss to coat. Add orange slices, grapefruit slices, and clementine segments. Lightly toss to mix. Arrange salad on a platter. Sprinkle with toasted coconut.

FOR 12 SERVINGS In Step 1 squeeze juice from two oranges.

PER SERVING *211 cal., 15 g fat (7 g sat. fat), 0 mg chol., 67 mg sodium, 19 g carb., 5 g fiber, 3 g pro.*

PREP 20 minutes

6 servings	ingredients	12 servings
3	oranges	6
¼ cup	extra-virgin olive oil	½ cup
1 Tbsp.	snipped fresh tarragon	2 Tbsp.
1 Tbsp.	Dijon mustard	2 Tbsp.
2 heads	Bibb lettuce, torn	4 heads
1	pink grapefruit, peeled and thinly sliced	2
2	clementines, peeled and separated into segments	4
½ cup	unsweetened flaked coconut, toasted (see tip, page 24)	1 cup

Kohlrabi-Carrot Salad with Dill Vinaigrette

Kohlrabi may be the ugliest vegetable you'll ever love. It looks a bit like a bumpy space capsule and has a crisp, juicy texture and mild cabbage flavor that lends itself to preparations both raw and cooked.

1. For the Dill Vinaigrette, in a screw-top jar combine vinegar, oil, sugar, dill, celery seeds, salt, and black pepper. Cover and shake well to combine.

2. In a large bowl combine kohlrabi, sweet pepper, carrot, and shallot. Add vinaigrette; toss gently to coat.

3. Cover and chill salad for 2 hours, stirring occasionally to coat with dressing. Stir before serving. Sprinkle with fresh dill, if desired.

*TIP If desired, for 6 servings, substitute ¼ teaspoon dried dill for the fresh dill. For 12 servings, substitute ½ teaspoon dried dill for the fresh dill.

**TIP If desired, for 6 servings substitute 3 cups chopped green cabbage for the kohlrabi. For 12 servings, substitute 6 cups chopped green cabbage for the kohlrabi.

PER SERVING 48 cal., 2 g fat (0 g sat. fat), 0 mg chol., 73 mg sodium, 7 g carb., 3 g fiber, 2 g pro.

PREP 20 minutes
CHILL 2 hours

6 servings	ingredients	12 servings
¼ cup	cider vinegar	½ cup
2 Tbsp.	olive oil	¼ cup
1 tsp.	sugar	2 tsp.
1 tsp.	snipped fresh dill*	2 tsp.
¼ tsp.	celery seeds	½ tsp.
⅛ tsp.	salt	¼ tsp.
⅛ tsp.	black pepper	¼ tsp.
4 medium (3 cups)	kohlrabi,** peeled and chopped	8 medium (6 cups)
1 medium	red and/or green sweet pepper, cut into bite-size strips	2 medium
½ cup	coarsely chopped carrot	1 cup
1	medium shallot, thinly sliced	2
	Fresh dill (optional)	

Creamy Broccoli Salad

The sweetness of raisins combined with smoky, salty bacon—plus refreshingly crunchy texture of broccoli—make this popular potluck salad irresistible.

1. In a large bowl combine mayonnaise, raisins, onion, sugar, and vinegar. Stir in broccoli. Cover and chill for 2 to 24 hours. Before serving, stir in sunflower kernels and bacon.

PER SERVING *247 cal., 20 g fat (4 g sat. fat), 13 mg chol., 242 mg sodium, 13 g carb., 2 g fiber, 5 g pro.*

PREP 20 minutes
CHILL 2 hours

12 servings	ingredients	24 servings
1 cup	mayonnaise	2 cups
½ cup	raisins	1 cup
¼ cup	finely chopped red onion	½ cup
3 Tbsp.	sugar	6 Tbsp.
2 Tbsp.	vinegar	¼ cup
7 cups	chopped broccoli florets	14 cups
½ cup	sunflower kernels	1 cup
8 slices	bacon, crisp-cooked, drained, and crumbled	16 slices

Fresh Corn Salad with Summer Herbs

Serve this summery salad made with raw sweet corn in an herbed vinaigrette with grilled steak or pork chops.

PREP 20 minutes
STAND 30 minutes

4 servings	ingredients	8 servings
4	ears of corn, husks and silks removed	8
3 Tbsp.	snipped fresh herbs, such as chives, sage, oregano, cilantro, parsley, and/or basil	6 Tbsp.
2 Tbsp.	chopped red onion or shallot	¼ cup
1 Tbsp.	olive oil	2 Tbsp.
2 tsp.	red wine vinegar or other vinegar	4 tsp.
¼ tsp.	sea salt or salt	½ tsp.
⅛ tsp.	freshly ground black pepper	¼ tsp.
⅛ tsp.	crushed red pepper	¼ tsp.

1. Carefully cut corn kernels off cobs. Place corn in a medium bowl. Stir in herbs, onion, oil, vinegar, salt, black pepper, and crushed red pepper. Let stand at room temperature for 30 minutes before serving.

PER SERVING *110 cal., 4 g fat (1 g sat. fat), 0 mg chol., 114 mg sodium, 18 g carb., 3 g fiber, 3 g pro.*

Spicy Green Stir-Fry with Peanuts

Easily adapt this healthful recipe to a main dish: Stir-fry 12 ounces of sliced chicken breast for 4 servings or 1½ pounds sliced chicken breast for 8 servings before beginning Step 1. Set the chicken aside, then add it to the vegetables in the wok in Step 3, right before the sauce is added.

1. For sauce, in a small bowl stir together the water, teriyaki sauce, and cornstarch; set aside.

2. Pour half the oil into a wok or large nonstick skillet; heat wok over medium-high heat. Add ginger; cook and stir for 15 seconds. Add peanuts; cook and stir for 30 seconds. Transfer peanuts to a small bowl. Immediately sprinkle with cayenne pepper; toss gently to coat.

3. Add the remaining oil to wok. Add green beans; cook and stir for 3 minutes. Add sweet pepper, edamame, and garlic; cook and stir for 3 to 5 minutes or until vegetables are crisp-tender. Stir sauce; add to vegetables in wok. Cook and stir until thickened and bubbly. Cook and stir for 2 minutes more. Stir in bok choy. Top with peanuts.

*TIP If desired, for 4 servings, you may substitute 3 cups coarsely shredded napa cabbage for the bok choy. For 8 servings, you may substitute 6 cups coarsely shredded napa cabbage for the bok choy.

PER SERVING *130 cal., 9 g fat (1 g sat. fat), 0 mg chol., 142 mg sodium, 8 g carb., 3 g fiber, 6 g pro.*

START TO FINISH **25 minutes**

4 servings	ingredients	8 servings
¼ cup	cold water	½ cup
1 Tbsp.	light teriyaki sauce	2 Tbsp.
½ tsp.	cornstarch	1 tsp.
2 tsp.	peanut oil or toasted sesame oil	4 tsp.
1 tsp.	grated fresh ginger	2 tsp.
⅓ cup	lightly salted peanuts	⅔ cup
⅛ tsp.	cayenne pepper or crushed red pepper	¼ tsp.
4 oz. (¾ cup)	fresh green beans, trimmed (if desired)	8 oz. (1½ cups)
½ large	green or red sweet pepper cut into thin bite-size strips	1 large
⅓ cup	frozen shelled sweet soybeans (edamame), thawed	⅔ cup
1 clove	garlic, minced	2 cloves
2	baby bok choy, separated into leaves*	4

Mediterranean Broccoli Medley

A vibrant blend of vegetables is cooked to a crisp-tender texture, then tossed with a vinaigrette and topped with feta cheese and served warm.

1. Bring a large Dutch oven of water to boiling. Add broccoli, mushrooms, carrots, and summer squash to boiling water. Return to boiling. Cook for 1 to 2 minutes or just until crisp-tender; drain. Return vegetables to Dutch oven.

2. For vinaigrette, in a small bowl whisk together vinegar, olive oil, pepper, mustard, and salt. Add vinaigrette and basil to the cooked vegetables; toss to combine. Transfer vegetables to a serving bowl; sprinkle with feta cheese.

PER SERVING *64 cal., 3 g fat (1 g sat. fat), 2 mg chol., 205 mg sodium, 7 g carb., 2 g fiber, 4 g pro.*

START TO FINISH 25 minutes

8 servings	ingredients	16 servings
4 cups	fresh broccoli florets	8 cups
8 oz.	sliced fresh cremini or button mushrooms	16 oz.
1 cup	thinly bias-sliced carrots	2 cups
1 cup	coarsely chopped yellow summer squash	2 cups
1 Tbsp.	white balsamic vinegar or white wine vinegar	2 Tbsp.
1 Tbsp.	olive oil	2 Tbsp.
½ tsp.	black pepper	1 tsp.
½ tsp.	Dijon mustard	1 tsp.
¼ tsp.	salt	½ tsp.
⅓ cup	snipped fresh basil	⅔ cup
½ cup (2 oz.)	crumbled reduced-fat feta cheese	1 cup (4 oz.)

Saucy Skillet Mushrooms

For a different sort of side, try these mushrooms flavored with bacon and stone-ground mustard. They're outstanding with steak!

1. In a large heavy skillet cook bacon over medium heat until crisp. Using a slotted spoon, remove bacon and drain on paper towels, reserving drippings in skillet.

2. Add oil to the reserved drippings. Add mushrooms; cook and stir over medium heat for 1 to 2 minutes or just until mushrooms begin to brown. Cook, covered, about 8 minutes or until tender, stirring occasionally. Stir in mustard; heat through. To serve, sprinkle with crumbled bacon and parsley.

PER SERVING *214 cal., 19 g fat (6 g sat. fat), 25 mg chol., 356 mg sodium, 4 g carb., 1 g fiber, 8 g pro.*

START TO FINISH **20 minutes**

4 servings	ingredients	8 servings
4 slices	bacon, chopped	8 slices
1 Tbsp.	olive oil	2 Tbsp.
1 lb.	large button mushrooms, stems removed (1½ to 2 inches in diameter)	2 lb.
2 Tbsp.	stone-ground mustard	¼ cup
2 Tbsp.	snipped fresh flat-leaf parsley	¼ cup

Oven-Roasted Brussels Sprouts with Apples, Cherries, and Pecans

Even Brussels sprouts skeptics will be won over by these caramelized sprouts flavored with sweet apples and dried cherries and tossed with crunchy pecans.

PREP 10 minutes
ROAST 20 minutes at 425°F

4 servings	ingredients	8 servings
1 lb.	Brussels sprouts	2 lb.
2 Tbsp.	olive oil	¼ cup
½ tsp.	kosher salt	1 tsp.
⅛ tsp.	cayenne pepper	¼ tsp.
1 cup	sliced or coarsely chopped apple	2 cups
½ cup	dried cherries or cranberries	1 cup
¼ cup	chopped pecans	½ cup
¼ cup	bottled red wine vinaigrette or desired vinaigrette	½ cup

1. Preheat oven to 425°F. Line a 15×10×1-inch baking pan with foil; set aside. Trim stems and remove any wilted outer leaves from Brussels sprouts. Halve sprouts lengthwise.

2. Place Brussels sprouts in the prepared baking pan. Drizzle with oil and sprinkle with salt and cayenne pepper; toss well to combine.

3. Roast, uncovered, for 15 minutes. Stir in apple, dried cherries, and pecans. Roast, uncovered, for 5 to 10 minutes more or until sprouts are crisp-tender and lightly browned. Drizzle with vinaigrette; toss gently to coat.

PER SERVING *250 cal., 15 g fat (2 g sat. fat), 0 mg chol., 389 mg sodium, 32 g carb., 6 g fiber, 5 g pro.*

Fingerling Potato Salad with Honey-Thyme Vinaigrette

Haricots verts is simply French for "green string beans." You can find them specifically labeled as such—or use very young regular green beans.

PREP 30 minutes   COOK 9 minutes
STAND 5 minutes   CHILL 2 hours

8 servings	ingredients	16 servings
1½ lb.	white or yellow fingerling potatoes	3 lb.
1 tsp.	kosher salt	2 tsp.
8 oz.	fresh haricots verts or tender young green beans	1 lb.
3 cups	water	6 cups
¼ cup	cider vinegar	½ cup
1	medium shallot, halved	2
2 Tbsp.	honey	¼ cup
1 Tbsp.	fresh thyme leaves	2 Tbsp.
1½ tsp.	Dijon mustard	1 Tbsp.
⅛ tsp.	kosher salt	¼ tsp.
⅛ tsp.	black pepper	¼ tsp.
½ cup	canola or vegetable oil	1 cup
1	small red onion, halved and thinly sliced	2
1 lb.	bacon, crisp-cooked, drained and crumbled	2 lb.
½ cup	crumbled feta cheese	1 cup

1. Scrub potatoes. In a large saucepan cook potatoes with the 1 teaspoon kosher salt, covered, in enough boiling water to cover for 8 to 10 minutes or just until tender; drain well. Spread in a single layer in a shallow baking pan to cool. When cool enough to handle, halve potatoes lengthwise. Set aside.

2. Wash haricots verts; trim and, if desired, halve crosswise. In a medium saucepan bring the 3 cups water to boiling. Add haricots verts. Return to boiling. Simmer, uncovered, for 1 to 2 minutes or just until crisp-tender. Immediately remove haricots verts from boiling water with a slotted spoon; plunge into a large bowl half-filled with ice water. Let stand for 5 minutes; drain well. Set aside.

3. For the vinaigrette, in a food processor or blender combine vinegar, shallot, honey, thyme, mustard, the ⅛ teaspoon kosher salt, and the pepper. Cover and process or blend until combined. With processor or blender running, slowly add oil in a steady stream until vinaigrette is thickened.

4. In a large salad bowl combine potatoes, haricots verts, and red onion. Drizzle with enough of the vinaigrette to thoroughly coat. Cover and chill for 2 to 24 hours.

5. Just before serving, toss salad with bacon and top with feta cheese. Serve with remaining vinaigrette or reserve vinaigrette for another use.

FOR 16 SERVINGS In Step 1 cook potatoes with 2 teaspoons kosher salt. In Step 3 use the ¼ teaspoon kosher salt.

PER SERVING *324 cal., 22 g fat (4 g sat. fat), 24 mg chol., 753 mg sodium, 23 g carb., 3 g fiber, 9 g pro.*

Mashed Sweet Potatoes with Mushrooms and Bacon

The term "sweet potatoes" refers to both orange- and yellow-flesh tubers. The orange-flesh variety is sweeter and has a slightly creamier texture than the yellow-flesh variety.

1. Peel sweet potatoes; cut into 2-inch pieces. In a covered 4- to 5-quart Dutch oven cook potatoes in enough boiling, lightly salted water to cover for 20 to 25 minutes or until tender.

2. Meanwhile, while potatoes are cooking, in a large skillet cook bacon over medium heat until crisp. Remove bacon and drain on paper towels, reserving 3 tablespoons drippings in skillet. Crumble bacon; set aside. Add mushrooms and onion to the reserved drippings. Cook over medium heat about 8 minutes or until mushrooms are tender and browned, stirring occasionally. Stir in crumbled bacon, raisins, and lemon juice.

3. Drain potatoes; return to Dutch oven. Mash potatoes with a potato masher or beat with a mixer on low. Add milk, butter, and salt. Stir or beat until butter is melted and potatoes are light and fluffy.

3. To serve, transfer mashed potatoes to a serving bowl. Top with mushroom mixture.

TO MAKE AHEAD: Prepare as directed in Step 1 and Step 3. Transfer mashed potatoes to an airtight container. Cover and chill up to 24 hours. To serve, transfer mashed potatoes to a large saucepan; heat through. Continue as directed in Step 2.

FOR 20 SERVINGS In Step 1 use a 6- to 8-quart Dutch oven. In Step 2 reserve 6 tablespoons drippings.

PER SERVING *196 cal., 8 g fat (4 g sat. fat), 15 mg chol., 364 mg sodium, 27 g carb., 4 g fiber, 5 g pro.*

START TO FINISH **30 minutes**

10 servings	ingredients	20 servings
3 lb.	orange-flesh sweet potatoes	6 lb.
½ cup	milk	1 cup
2 Tbsp.	butter	¼ cup
1 tsp.	kosher salt	2 tsp.
6 slices	bacon	12 slices
8 oz.	fresh cremini mushrooms, halved (quarter any large mushrooms)	1 lb.
1	large red onion, cut into thin wedges	2
⅓ cup	golden raisins	⅔ cup
2 Tbsp.	lemon juice	¼ cup

Cheesy Cauliflower

Try the creamy cheese sauce with broccoli as well—or a blend of broccoli and cauliflower.

1. In a large saucepan combine cauliflower, 1¼ cups of the milk, and the salt. Bring to boiling; reduce heat. Simmer, covered, for 6 to 8 minutes or until cauliflower is crisp-tender.

2. Meanwhile, in a small bowl whisk together flour and the remaining milk until smooth. Stir flour mixture into cauliflower. Cook and stir until thickened. Stir in cheese, mustard, and pepper until cheese is melted. Transfer to a serving dish. If desired, sprinkle with snipped fresh chives.

FOR 8 SERVINGS In Step 1, use 2½ cups of the milk.

PER SERVING *142 cal., 7 g fat (4 g sat. fat), 22 mg chol., 538 mg sodium, 13 g carb., 2 g fiber, 9 g pro.*

START TO FINISH 25 minutes

4 servings	ingredients	8 servings
4 cups	cauliflower florets	8 cups
1½ cups	milk	3 cups
½ tsp.	salt	1 tsp.
2 Tbsp.	all-purpose flour	¼ cup
½ cup (2 oz.)	shredded sharp cheddar cheese	1 cup (4 oz.)
1 Tbsp.	Dijon mustard	2 Tbsp.
⅛ tsp.	ground white pepper	¼ tsp.
	Snipped fresh chives (optional)	

Creamy Coleslaw

If someone puts you in charge of the coleslaw for the extended family reunion, this economical, big-yield recipe is the perfect choice.

1. In an extra-large bowl combine green cabbage, red cabbage, and carrots.

2. For the dressing, in a small bowl combine mayonnaise, sour cream, sugar, vinegar, mustard, salt, and pepper. Stir dressing into coleslaw. Cover and chill for 2 hours before serving.

PER SERVING *84 cal., 7 g fat (2 g sat. fat), 5 mg chol., 128 mg sodium, 5 g carb., 1 g fiber, 1 g pro.*

PREP 30 minutes
CHILL 2 hours

11 servings	ingredients	22 servings
1 medium head (about 9 cups)	green cabbage, cut into ¼- to ½-inch strips	2 medium heads (about 18 cups)
½ small head (about 3 cups)	red cabbage, cut into ¼- to ½-inch strips	1 small head (about 6 cups)
1 cup	shredded carrots	2 cups
¾ cup	mayonnaise	1½ cups
½ cup	sour cream	1 cup
2 Tbsp.	sugar	¼ cup
1 Tbsp.	cider vinegar	2 Tbsp.
1 Tbsp.	Dijon mustard	2 Tbsp.
½ tsp.	salt	1 tsp.
½ tsp.	black pepper	1 tsp.

Beans with Blue Cheese

For a special holiday meal, these bacon-and-blue-cheese green beans are a nice change of pace from classic green bean casserole.

1. Place fresh green beans in a steamer basket in a saucepan. Add water to saucepan to just below the basket. Bring to boiling. Steam, covered, for 8 to 10 minutes or until beans are crisp-tender. (Or cook frozen beans according to package directions; drain.)

2. Meanwhile, in a large skillet cook bacon over medium heat until crisp. Remove bacon and drain on paper towels, reserving drippings in skillet. Crumble bacon; set aside.

3. Add onion to the reserved drippings. Cook over medium heat until tender, stirring occasionally. Stir in lemon juice. Stir in beans; heat through. Add crumbled bacon and cheese. Cook and stir about 1 minute more or until cheese begins to melt. Sprinkle with walnuts.

*TIP If desired, for 4 servings, use two 9-ounce packages frozen French-cut green bean instead of fresh green beans. For 8 servings, use four 9-ounce packages frozen French-cut green beans instead of fresh green beans.

PER SERVING *220 cal., 16 g fat (4 g sat. fat), 14 mg chol., 279 mg sodium, 14 g carb., 4 g fiber, 9 g pro.*

START TO FINISH 20 minutes

4 servings	ingredients	8 servings
1 lb.	fresh green beans*	2 lb.
3 slices	bacon	6 slices
½ cup	chopped onion	1 cup
2 tsp.	lemon juice	4 tsp.
½ cup (2 oz.)	crumbled blue cheese	1 cup (4 oz.)
½ cup	walnut pieces, toasted (see tip, page 24)	1 cup

Baked Cheese Grits

Be sure to get quick-cooking—not instant—grits for this homey casserole.

PREP 15 minutes
BAKE 30 minutes at 325°F
STAND 5 minutes

4 servings	ingredients	8 servings
2	eggs	4
4 cups	chicken broth	8 cups
1 cup	quick-cooking grits	2 cups
2 cups	shredded cheddar cheese	4 cups
¼ cup	sliced green onion	½ cup
2 Tbsp.	butter	¼ cup
1 cup	chopped tomato (optional)	2 cups
	Sliced green onion (optional)	

1. Preheat oven to 325°F. In a small bowl lightly beat the eggs. In a medium saucepan bring broth to boiling. Slowly add grits, stirring constantly. Gradually stir about 1 cup of the hot grits into egg; return to saucepan. Remove from heat. Stir in cheese, the ¼ cup green onions, and the butter until cheese and butter are melted.

2. Pour grits into an ungreased 1-quart casserole. Bake for 30 to 35 minutes or until a knife inserted near center comes out clean. Let stand for 5 minutes before serving. If desired, top with tomato and additional green onion.

FOR 8 SERVINGS In Step 1, gradually stir about 2 cups of the hot grits into the eggs, and use ½ cup sliced green onions. In Step 2, use an ungreased 2-quart casserole.

PER SERVING *238 cal., 14 g fat (8 g sat. fat), 91 mg chol., 694 mg sodium, 17 g carb., 0 g fiber, 11 g pro.*

Cheesy Mexican Polenta

Queso Chihuahua is a soft mild cow's milk cheese that is most often sold in braids, balls, or rounds. It has excellent melting qualities, similar to mild cheddar or Monterey Jack.

1. In a Dutch oven combine 2¼ cups of the milk, the broth, canned chile peppers, garlic powder, oregano, and salt. Bring to boiling. Gradually add polenta mix, stirring constantly. Reduce heat to low.

2. Cook, uncovered, for 5 to 10 minutes or until thickened. Stir in corn and cheese. Stir in enough of the remaining milk to reach desired consistency. Remove from heat. Let stand for 5 minutes before serving. If desired, top with additional cheese and chopped jalapeño.

FOR 16 SERVINGS In Step 1 use 4½ cups of the milk.

PER SERVING *164 cal., 5 g fat (3 g sat. fat), 18 mg chol., 472 mg sodium, 23 g carb., 2 g fiber, 7 g pro.*

START TO FINISH 20 minutes

8 servings	ingredients	16 servings
2¼ to 2¾ cups	milk	4½ to 5½ cups
one 14.5-oz. can	chicken broth	two 14.5-oz. cans
one 4-oz. can	diced green chile peppers, undrained	two 4-oz. cans
1 tsp.	garlic powder	2 tsp.
1 tsp.	dried oregano, crushed	2 tsp.
½ tsp.	salt	1 tsp.
1 cup	quick-cooking polenta mix or coarse ground cornmeal	2 cups
1 cup	frozen whole kernel corn	2 cups
¾ cup (3 oz.)	shredded queso Chihuahua or mild cheddar cheese	1½ cups (6 oz.)
	shredded queso Chihuahua or mild cheddar cheese (optional)	
	chopped jalapeño (optional)	

Italian Pesto Pasta Salad

Prepared pesto comes in shelf-stable jars and, in some stores, also in the refrigerated section. Refrigerated pesto has a slightly fresher flavor and brighter green color than the jarred variety—although either type works well in this salad.

1. Cook macaroni according to package directions. Drain and rinse well under cold water; set aside.

2. In a large bowl stir together pesto, vinegar, and salt. Add beans, cooked macaroni, arugula, half the cheese, and half the pine nuts. Toss well. Serve immediately or cover and chill up to 6 hours. Top with remaining cheese and pine nuts before serving.

PER SERVING *244 cal., 12 g fat (3 g sat. fat), 5 mg chol., 474 mg sodium, 25 g carb., 3 g fiber, 9 g pro.*

PREP 30 minutes

10 servings	ingredients	20 servings
8 oz.	dried elbow macaroni	16 oz.
one 7- to 8-oz. jar	purchased basil pesto	two 7- to 8-oz. jars
¼ cup	red wine vinegar	½ cup
½ tsp.	kosher salt	1 tsp.
two 15-oz. cans	cannellini beans, rinsed and drained	four 15-oz. cans
half 5-oz. pkg. (3 cups)	baby arugula	one 5-oz. pkg. (6 cups)
2 oz.	Parmigiano-Reggiano cheese, shaved	4 oz.
¼ cup	pine nuts, toasted (see tip, page 24)	½ cup

Thai Coconut and Basmati Rice

Try this sweet-and-savory rice with steamed, baked, or grilled fish.

1. In a medium saucepan heat the oil over medium heat. Add onion; cook for 5 to 7 minutes or until tender. Stir in rice. Cook and stir for 1 minute more. Stir in coconut milk, broth, the water, salt, and pepper. Bring to boiling; reduce heat. Simmer, covered, about 20 minutes or until rice is tender and liquid is absorbed. If desired, stir in mango and basil.

PER SERVING *137 cal., 5 g fat (3 g sat. fat), 0 mg chol., 190 mg sodium, 21 g carb., 0 g fiber, 3 g pro.*

PREP 20 minutes
COOK 26 minutes

4 servings	ingredients	8 servings
2 tsp.	olive oil	4 tsp.
½ cup	chopped onion	1 cup
½ cup	basmati rice	1 cup
¾ cup	unsweetened light coconut milk	1½ cups
¼ cup	reduced-sodium chicken broth	½ cup
¼ cup	water	½ cup
¼ tsp.	salt	½ tsp.
¼ tsp.	black pepper	½ tsp.
1	medium mango, halved, seeded, peeled, and chopped (optional)	2
¼ cup	snipped fresh basil (optional)	½ cup

Chili-Cheese Corn Bread

Although using vegetable oil is faster and doesn't contribute any saturated fat to the corn bread, melted butter infuses the bread with more flavor.

1. Preheat oven to 400°F. In a medium bowl stir together flour, cornmeal, sugar, baking powder, and salt. Make a well in the center of flour mixture; set aside.

2. Place the 1 tablespoon butter in a 10-inch cast iron skillet or 8×8×2-inch baking pan. Place skillet in the oven for 3 minutes or until butter is melted. Remove from oven; swirl butter to coat bottom and sides of pan.

3. Meanwhile, in a small bowl combine eggs, milk, and oil. Add egg mixture all at once to flour mixture; stir just until moistened (batter should be lumpy). Fold in cheese, chile peppers, and chili powder. Pour batter into the hot pan, spreading evenly.

4. Bake for 15 to 20 minutes or until a wooden toothpick inserted near the center comes out clean. Cool slightly in pan on a wire rack. Serve warm.

PER SERVING *279 cal., 15 g fat (5 g sat. fat), 72 mg chol., 454 mg sodium, 28 g carb., 1 g fiber, 9 g pro.*

PREP 20 minutes
BAKE 15 minutes at 400°F

8 servings	ingredients	16 servings
1 cup	all-purpose flour	2 cups
¾ cup	cornmeal	1½ cups
2 to 3 Tbsp.	sugar	4 to 6 Tbsp.
2½ tsp.	baking powder	5 tsp.
¾ tsp.	salt	1½ tsp.
1 Tbsp.	butter	2 Tbsp.
2	eggs, lightly beaten	4
1 cup	milk	2 cups
¼ cup	vegetable oil or butter, melted	½ cup
1 cup (4 oz.)	shredded Monterey Jack cheese	2 cups (8 oz.)
one 4-oz. can	diced green chile peppers, drained	two 4-oz. cans
1 to 2 tsp.	chili powder	2 to 4 tsp.

Sage and Pepper Popovers

6 servings	ingredients	12 servings
1 Tbsp.	shortening or nonstick cooking spray	2 Tbsp.
2	eggs, lightly beaten	4
1 cup	milk	2 cups
1 Tbsp.	olive oil	2 Tbsp.
1 cup	all-purpose flour	2 cups
2 Tbsp.	grated Parmesan cheese	¼ cup
2 tsp.	finely snipped fresh sage or thyme*	4 tsp.
½ tsp.	salt	1 tsp.
½ tsp.	freshly ground black pepper	1 tsp.

Airy, custardy popovers are as much fun to make as they are to eat. It's magical watching them puff up in the oven. Prick them with a fork when they come out of the oven to allow the steam to escape, which prevents them from collapsing as they cool. They're wonderful with roast beef.

1. Preheat oven to 400°F. Using ½ teaspoon shortening for each cup, grease the bottoms and sides of six popover pan cups or 6-ounce custard cups. (Or lightly coat with cooking spray.) If using custard cups, place cups in a 15×10×1-inch baking pan; set aside.

2. In a medium bowl combine eggs, milk, and oil. Stir in flour until smooth. Stir in cheese, sage, salt, and pepper.

3. Fill the prepared cups half full with batter. Bake for 40 minutes or until very firm.

4. Immediately after removing from oven, prick each popover with a fork to let steam escape. Turn off oven. For crisper popovers, return to oven for 5 to 10 minutes or until popovers reach desired crispness. Remove popovers from cups. Serve immediately.

*TIP If desired, for 6 servings, use ½ teaspoon dried sage or thyme, crushed, in place of the 2 teaspoons fresh sage or thyme. For 12 servings, use 1 teaspoon dried sage or thyme, crushed, in place of the 4 teaspoons fresh sage or thyme.

FOR 12 SERVINGS In Step 1, use 12 popover pan cups or 6-ounce custard cups.

PER SERVING *153 cal., 7 g fat (2 g sat. fat), 74 mg chol., 237 mg sodium, 17 g carb., 1 g fiber, 5 g pro.*

CHAPTER 6

Desserts

Whether you are looking for just a nibble of something sweet—or for a rich, gooey, indulgent treat—you'll find the perfect ending here.

169

171

187

Blueberry-Nut Streusel Coffee Cake

Serve this as dessert—or with an egg casserole and fresh fruit for a special-occasion brunch.

1. Preheat oven to 350°F. For topping, in a medium bowl combine brown sugar, nuts, and cinnamon; set aside. In a small bowl stir together sour cream and baking soda; set aside. Grease an 8×8×2-inch baking pan.

2. In a large mixing bowl beat granulated sugar and softened butter with a mixer on medium for 2 minutes or until well mixed. Add vanilla and eggs, one at a time, beating well after each addition. Beat in flour and baking powder; beat until well combined. Add the foamy sour cream mixture; beat until well combined.

3. Spread half the batter in the prepared pan. Evenly sprinkle blueberries and all but ½ cup of the topping on the batter. Spread the remaining batter on topping. Sprinkle remaining topping on batter.

4. Bake for 35 to 40 minutes or until a toothpick inserted near the center comes out clean. Cool for 30 minutes before drizzling with powdered sugar icing.

5. Meanwhile, for powdered sugar icing, in a small bowl combine powdered sugar, milk, and vanilla. Stir in enough additional milk, 1 teaspoon at a time, to make icing of drizzling consistency.

FOR 16 SERVINGS In Step 1 grease a 10-inch tube pan or 13×9×2-inch baking pan. In Step 3 sprinkle all but 1 cup of the topping over the batter. In Step 4, for a tube pan, cool for 1 hour before removing cake from pan; drizzle with powdered sugar icing. For a 13×9×2-inch baking pan, cool for 30 minutes before drizzling with powdered sugar icing.

PER SERVING *347 cal., 14 g fat (6 g sat. fat), 58 mg chol., 195 mg sodium, 52 g carb., 2 g fiber, 4 g pro.*

PREP 30 minutes
BAKE 35 minutes at 350°F
COOL 30 minutes

8 servings	ingredients	16 servings
¾ cup	packed brown sugar	1½ cups
½ cup	coarsely chopped walnuts	1 cup
1 tsp.	ground cinnamon	2 tsp.
half 8-oz. carton	sour cream	one 8-oz. carton
½ tsp.	baking soda	1 tsp.
6 Tbsp.	granulated sugar	¾ cup
¼ cup	butter, softened	½ cup
½ tsp.	vanilla extract	1 tsp.
2	eggs	3
1 cup	all-purpose flour	2 cups
¾ tsp.	baking powder	1½ tsp.
1 cup	fresh or frozen blueberries, thawed	2 cups
6 Tbsp.	powdered sugar	¾ cup
1½ tsp.	milk	1 Tbsp.
¼ tsp.	vanilla	½ tsp.

Chocolate Picnic Cake

PREP 20 minutes
bake 30 minutes at 350°F

6 servings	ingredients	12 servings
¾ cup	sugar	1½ cups
4½ tsp.	unsweetened cocoa powder	3 Tbsp.
dash	salt	⅛ tsp.
¼ cup	whipping cream	½ cup
2 Tbsp.	milk	¼ cup
1½ tsp.	vanilla	1 Tbsp.
½ cup	chopped walnuts	1 cup
½ cup	semisweet chocolate pieces	1 cup
¼ cup	sugar	½ cup
1 cup + 2 Tbsp.	all-purpose flour	2¼ cups
¾ cup	sugar	1½ cups
3 Tbsp.	unsweetened cocoa powder	⅓ cup
¾ tsp.	baking soda	1½ tsp.
¼ tsp.	salt	½ tsp.
¾ cup	strong-brewed coffee, cooled or water	1½ cups
½ cup	canola oil	1 cup
2¼ tsp.	vinegar	4½ tsp.
¾ tsp.	vanilla	1½ tsp.
	Vanilla ice cream (optional)	

Opting for strong-brewed coffee instead of water gives this cake yummy mocha flavor.

1. Preheat oven to 350°F. Grease and flour an 8×8×2-inch baking pan; set aside. For the chocolate sauce, in a heavy saucepan combine ¾ cup sugar, the 4½ teaspoons cocoa powder, and dash salt. Stir in whipping cream and milk. Bring to a gentle boil, stirring constantly; reduce heat. Cook and stir for 2 minutes. Remove from heat; stir in the 1½ teaspoons vanilla. Transfer to a bowl; cover surface with plastic wrap. Cool to room temperature.

2. For picnic topping, in a small bowl combine walnuts, chocolate pieces, and ¼ cup sugar; set aside.

3. In a large mixing bowl stir together flour, ¾ cup sugar, the 3 tablespoons cocoa powder, baking soda, and the ¼ teaspoon salt. Stir in the coffee or water, oil, vinegar and ¾ teaspoon vanilla. Beat batter with a fork until smooth. Pour into prepared pan. Sprinkle with picnic topping.

4. Bake for 30 to 40 minutes or until a wooden toothpick inserted near center comes out clean. Cool cake slightly in pan on a wire rack. Serve warm with a scoop of vanilla ice cream, if desired, and drizzle with chocolate sauce.

FOR 12 SERVINGS In Step 1 use a 13×9×2-inch baking pan. For the chocolate sauce, use 1½ cups sugar, 3 tablespoons unsweetened cocoa powder, ⅛ teaspoon salt, and 1 tablespoon vanilla. In Step 2, for picnic topping, use ½ cup sugar. In Step 3 use ½ cups sugar, ⅓ cup unsweetened cocoa powder, ½ teaspoon salt, and 1½ teaspoons vanilla.

PER SERVING *722 cal., 32 g fat (11 g sat. fat), 46 mg chol., 334 mg sodium, 107 g carb., 4 g fiber, 8 g pro.*

Cinnamon-Orange Pumpkin Bread Pudding

In a world gone mad for anything pumpkin spice, this autumnal dessert is sure to be a huge hit.

PREP 30 minutes
BAKE 1 hour at 350°F

8 servings	ingredients	16 servings
6 cups	pumpkin bread cubes*	12 cups
2	eggs, lightly beaten	4
2 cups	milk	4 cups
½ cup	granulated sugar	1 cup
¼ cup	butter, melted	½ cup
1 tsp.	finely shredded orange peel	2 tsp.
½ tsp.	pumpkin pie spice	1 tsp.
⅓ cup	tub-style cream cheese, softened	⅔ cup
1 Tbsp.	butter, softened	2 Tbsp.
3 Tbsp.	powdered sugar	6 Tbsp.
1 to 2 Tbsp.	orange juice	2 to 4 Tbsp.

1. Preheat oven to 350°F. Spread bread cubes in a single layer in a shallow baking pan. Bake for 20 to 30 minutes or until dry and lightly toasted; cool slightly.

2. Grease a 2-quart baking dish; set aside. In a large bowl combine eggs, milk, granulated sugar, melted butter, orange peel, and pumpkin pie spice. Stir in bread cubes until moistened. Transfer bread mixture to the prepared baking dish.

3. Bake for 40 to 45 minutes or until a knife inserted in the center comes out clean. Cool slightly on a wire rack.

4. Meanwhile, for icing, in a small mixing bowl beat cream cheese and the 1 tablespoon butter with a mixer on medium until combined. Beat in powdered sugar and 1 tablespoon of the orange juice until smooth. Beat in enough remaining orange juice, 1 teaspoon at a time, to reach drizzling consistency. To serve, drizzle icing over warm bread pudding.

*TIP For pumpkin bread, for 8 servings use a 1-pound loaf from a bakery, bake a loaf from a mix, or bake a loaf from scratch. For 16 servings, use a 2-pound loaf from a bakery, 2 loaves from a mix, or bake 2 loaves from scratch.

FOR 16 SERVINGS In Step 2 use a 3-quart baking dish. In Step 4 use 2 tablespoons butter and 2 tablespoons orange juice.

PER SERVING *369 cal., 18 g fat (7 g sat. fat), 89 mg chol., 393 mg sodium, 47 g carb., 1 g fiber, 7 g pro.*

Butterscotch Pudding with Crème Fraîche

Look for small tubs of crème fraîche in the specialty dairy section of your supermarket.

4 servings	ingredients	8 servings
½ cup	packed light brown sugar	1 cup
2 Tbsp.	cornstarch	¼ cup
⅛ tsp.	salt	¼ tsp.
2 cups	half-and-half or light cream	4 cups
3	egg yolks, lightly beaten	5
2 Tbsp.	butter, cut into small pieces	¼ cup
1 tsp.	vanilla	2 tsp.
¼ cup	crème fraîche	½ cup
1 Tbsp.	soft goat cheese (chèvre)	2 Tbsp.
1½ tsp.	sugar	1 Tbsp.
	Toffee pieces, chopped, and/or dried tart cherries (optional)	

1. In a medium saucepan combine brown sugar, cornstarch, and salt. Stir in half-and-half. Cook and stir over medium heat until thickened and bubbly. Cook and stir for 2 minutes more. Remove from heat.

2. Gradually stir about ½ cup of the hot mixture into egg yolks; return to half-and-half mixture in saucepan. Bring to a gentle boil; reduce heat. Cook and stir for 2 minutes. Remove from heat. Stir in butter and vanilla.

3. Pour pudding into a large bowl. Cover surface with plastic wrap. Chill for 4 to 5 hours or until completely chilled.

4. For the Crème Fraîche, in a small serving bowl combine crème fraîche, goat cheese, and sugar. Sprinkle Butterscotch Pudding with toffee pieces and/or cherries, if desired, and serve with Crème Fraîche.

FOR 8 SERVINGS In Step 2 gradually stir 1 cup of the hot mixture into egg yolks.

PER SERVING *429 cal., 29 g fat (17 g sat. fat), 212 mg chol., 194 mg sodium, 38 g carb., 0 g fiber, 6 g pro.*

Cranberry-Apple Crisp

The aroma of this apple-pie spice crisp baking in the oven on a cool fall day will warm you inside and out.

PREP 20 minutes
BAKE 40 minutes at 350°F
COOL 10 minutes

6 servings	ingredients	12 servings
½ cup	granulated sugar	1 cup
2 Tbsp.	snipped dried cranberries, dried cherries, or dried dates	¼ cup
1 tsp.	finely shredded lemon peel	2 tsp.
1 Tbsp.	lemon juice	2 Tbsp.
¾ tsp.	vanilla	1½ tsp.
3 cups	thinly sliced, peeled Granny Smith or cooking apples	6 cups
1 cup	fresh or frozen cranberries	2 cups
⅔ cup	rolled oats	1⅓ cups
⅓ cup	packed brown sugar	⅔ cup
2 Tbsp.	all-purpose flour	¼ cup
½ tsp.	apple pie spice	1 tsp.
¼ cup	chilled butter, cut into small pieces	½ cup
¼ cup	flaked coconut	½ cup
	Plain low-fat yogurt, half-and-half, or vanilla ice cream (optional)	

1. Preheat oven to 350°F. Grease an 8×8×2-inch baking dish or baking pan; set aside. In a large bowl combine granulated sugar, dried cranberries, lemon peel, lemon juice, and vanilla. Add sliced apples and fresh or frozen cranberries, gently tossing well to evenly coat. Place apple mixture in prepared dish.

2. For the topping, in a small bowl combine oats, brown sugar, flour, and apple pie spice. Using a pastry blender or two knives, cut in butter until topping resembles coarse crumbs. Stir in coconut. Sprinkle topping over apple mixture.

3. Bake for 40 to 45 minutes or until apples are tender and topping is golden. Cool on a wire rack for 10 minutes. Serve warm with yogurt, if desired.

FOR 12 SERVINGS In Step 1 use a 13×9×2-inch baking dish or baking pan.

PER SERVING *328 cal., 11 g fat (7 g sat. fat), 20 mg chol., 73 mg sodium, 57 g carb., 5 g fiber, 4 g pro.*

Rhubarb Cobbler

What's the difference between a cobbler and a crisp? A cobbler is topped with tender, flaky biscuits, while a crisp is topped with a blend of buttery crumbs made with flour, brown sugar, oats, and sometimes nuts.

1. Preheat oven to 400°F. For biscuit topper, in a medium bowl stir together flour, the 2 tablespoons sugar, baking powder, salt, and the ½ teaspoon cinnamon (if desired). Cut in butter until mixture resembles coarse crumbs; set aside.

2. For filling, in a large saucepan combine rhubarb, the 1 cup sugar, and the cornstarch. Cook over medium heat until rhubarb releases juices, stirring occasionally. Continue to cook, stirring constantly, over medium heat until thickened and bubbly. Keep the filling hot.

3. In a small bowl stir together egg and milk. Add to flour mixture, stirring just to moisten. Transfer hot filling to a 2-quart baking dish. Using a spoon, immediately drop batter into six mounds on top of filling. If desired, combine the 2 teaspoons sugar with ⅛ teaspoon cinnamon; sprinkle over biscuits.

4. Bake for 20 to 25 minutes or until biscuits are golden. Cool in dish on a wire rack for 30 minutes.

FOR 12 SERVINGS In Step 1 use the ¼ cup sugar and, if using, 1 teaspoon cinnamon. In Step , use the 2 cups sugar. In Step 3 use a 3-quart baking dish. If desired, combine the 4 teaspoons sugar with the ¼ teaspoon cinnamon; sprinkle over biscuits.

PER SERVING *400 cal., 9 g fat (5 g sat. fat), 52 mg chol., 309 mg sodium, 77 g carb., 3 g fiber, 5 g pro.*

PREP 30 minutes
BAKE 20 minutes at 400°F
COOL 30 minutes

6 servings	ingredients	12 servings
1 cup	all-purpose flour	2 cups
2 Tbsp.	sugar	¼ cup
1½ tsp.	baking powder	3 tsp.
¼ tsp.	salt	½ tsp.
½ tsp.	ground cinnamon (optional)	1 tsp.
¼ cup	butter	½ cup
6 cups	fresh or frozen unsweetened sliced rhubarb	12 cups
1 cup	sugar	2 cups
2 Tbsp.	cornstarch	¼ cup
1	egg	2
¼ cup	milk	½ cup
2 tsp.	sugar (optional)	4 tsp.
⅛ tsp.	ground cinnamon (optional)	¼ tsp.

White Chocolate, Coconut, and Pecan Brownies

If you can find vanilla bean paste, give it a try in these elegant brownies. (Use an equal amount of the paste in place of the vanilla extract.) Vanilla bean paste imparts beautiful flecks of vanilla bean seeds in baked goods.

PREP 30 minutes
BAKE 30 minutes at 350°F

20 servings	ingredients	40 servings
	Nonstick cooking spray	
½ cup	butter	1 cup
2 oz.	white baking chocolate with cocoa butter, chopped	4 oz.
2	eggs	4
⅔ cup	sugar	1⅓ cups
1 tsp.	vanilla	2 tsp.
1 cup	all-purpose flour	2 cups
½ tsp.	baking powder	1 tsp.
	Dash salt	
⅓ cup	white baking pieces	⅔ cup
⅓ cup	flaked coconut	⅔ cup
⅓ cup	chopped pecans, toasted (see tip, page 24)	⅔ cup
2 oz.	white baking chocolate with cocoa butter, melted	4 oz.

1. Preheat oven to 350°F. Line an 8×8×2-inch baking pan with foil, extending foil over edges of pan. Coat foil with cooking spray; set pan aside.

2. In a medium saucepan melt and stir butter and the chopped white chocolate over low heat until melted and smooth. Remove from heat. Add eggs, sugar, and vanilla. Beat lightly with a wooden spoon just until combined. In a small bowl stir together flour, baking powder, and salt. Add flour mixture to white chocolate mixture, stirring just until combined. Stir in white baking pieces, coconut, and pecans. Spread batter evenly in the prepared baking pan.

3. Bake for 30 to 35 minutes or until top is golden. Cool in pan on a wire rack. Using the edges of the foil, lift uncut brownies out of pan. Cut into bars. Drizzle with the melted white chocolate. Let stand until white chocolate is set.

FOR 40 SERVINGS In Step 1 use a 13×9×2-inch baking pan.

PER SERVING 165 cal., 10 g fat (6 g sat. fat), 33 mg chol., 81 mg sodium, 18 g carb., 0 g fiber, 2 g pro.

Cinnamon Bars

Serve these warmly spiced bars with a steaming mug of hot chocolate, hot tea, or coffee.

1. Preheat oven to 350°F. Line a 9×9×2-inch baking pan with foil, extending the foil over edges of pan. Grease foil; set pan aside. In a medium bowl stir together flour, 2 teaspoons of the cinnamon, the baking powder, and baking soda; set aside.

2. In a medium saucepan stir brown sugar and the ⅔ cup butter over medium heat until butter is melted and mixture is smooth. Remove from heat; cool slightly. Stir in eggs and vanilla. Stir in flour mixture until combined.

3. Pour batter into the prepared baking pan, spreading evenly. Bake for 25 to 30 minutes or until a wooden toothpick inserted near center comes out clean. Cool slightly in pan on a wire rack.

4. In a small bowl stir together granulated sugar and the remaining cinnamon. Brush warm bars with the 1 tablespoon melted butter then sprinkle with the cinnamon-sugar; cool completely. Using the edges of the foil, lift uncut bars from pan. Cut into bars.

FOR 48 SERVINGS In Step 1 use a 13×9×2-inch baking pan, and use 4 teaspoons of the cinnamon. In Step 2 use the 1⅓ cups butter. In Step 4 brush warm bars with 2 tablespoons melted butter.

PER SERVING *131 cal., 1 g fat (1 g sat. fat), 18 mg chol., 52 mg sodium, 28 g carb., 0 g fiber, 2 g pro.*

PREP 20 minutes
BAKE 25 minutes at 350°F

24 servings	ingredients	48 servings
2 cups	all-purpose flour	4 cups
3 tsp.	ground cinnamon	6 tsp.
1 tsp.	baking powder	2 tsp.
¼ tsp.	baking soda	½ tsp.
2 cups	packed brown sugar	4 cups
⅔ cup	butter	1⅓ cups
2	eggs	4
2 tsp.	vanilla	4 tsp.
¼ cup	granulated sugar	½ cup
1 Tbsp.	butter, melted	2 Tbsp.

Peach-Caramel Blondie Bars

So many good things come together in these over-the-top bars—white chocolate, caramel, juicy peaches, and salty pistachios.

PREP 20 minutes
BAKE 20 minutes at 325°F

16 servings	ingredients	32 servings
¾ cup	all-purpose flour	1½ cups
½ tsp.	baking powder	1 tsp.
¼ tsp.	salt	½ tsp.
¼ cup	butter, softened	½ cup
⅔ cup	sugar	1⅓ cups
1	egg	2
2 oz.	white baking chocolate, chopped	4 oz.
½ cup	dulce de leche or thick caramel-flavor ice cream topping	1 cup
2	small fresh peaches, pitted, and sliced	4
⅓ cup	pistachio nuts, coarsely chopped	⅔ cup

1. Preheat oven to 325°F. Line a 9×9×2-inch baking pan with foil, extending foil over edges of the pan. Grease foil; set aside.

2. For crust, in a medium bowl stir together flour, baking powder, and salt. Set aside. In a large bowl beat butter with a mixer on medium to high for 30 seconds. Add sugar. Beat for 5 minutes, scraping bowl occasionally. Add egg, beating well. Gradually add flour mixture, beating on low until combined. Spread evenly in prepared pan. Bake for 20 minutes or until crust is lightly browned and feels nearly firm in the center. Cool slightly on a wire rack.

3. In a small saucepan melt white chocolate over low heat. Spread evenly over the crust. Let stand until set (chill briefly if needed).

4. Use foil to lift uncut bars out of pan. Spread with dulce de leche. Cut into bars. Top with peaches; sprinkle with pistachios.

FOR 32 SERVINGS In Step 1 use a 13×9×2-inch baking pan.

PER SERVING *155 cal., 6 g fat (3 g sat. fat), 23 mg chol., 97 mg sodium, 23 g carb., 1 g fiber, 3 g pro.*

Cashew Crunch Bars

If you'd like, substitute salted roasted almonds for the cashews.

1. Preheat oven to 350°F. Line an 8×8×2-inch baking pan with foil, extending the foil over edges of pan. Grease foil; set pan aside.

2. For crust, in a large bowl stir together melted butter, brown sugar, vanilla, and baking powder. Stir in egg until combined. Stir in flour just until combined. Stir in toffee bits. Press mixture into the prepared baking pan. Bake for 20 to 25 minutes or until crust is lightly browned and center is set.

3. In a medium-size heavy saucepan melt caramels and milk over medium-low heat until mixture is smooth, stirring constantly. Carefully spread caramel over warm crust. Immediately sprinkle with cashews, pressing nuts gently into caramel. Cool in pan on a wire rack. Using the edges of the foil, lift uncut bars out of pan. Cut into bars.

FOR 24 SERVINGS In Step 1 use a 13×9×2-inch baking pan.

PER SERVING *280 cal., 14 g fat (7 g sat. fat), 24 mg chol., 205 mg sodium, 33 g carb., 1 g fiber, 4 g pro.*

PREP 20 minutes
BAKE 20 minutes at 350°F

12 servings	ingredients	24 servings
⅓ cup	butter, melted	¾ cup
⅓ cup	packed brown sugar	¾ cup
¾ tsp.	vanilla	1½ tsp.
¼ tsp.	baking powder	½ tsp.
1	egg, lightly beaten	2
1 cup	all-purpose flour	2 cups
¼ cup	almond toffee bits	½ cup
half 14-oz. pkg.	vanilla caramels, unwrapped	one 14-oz. pkg.
1 Tbsp.	milk or whipping cream	2 Tbsp.
1 cup	salted whole cashews, coarsely chopped	2 cups

Tangerine Cheesecake Bars

When you crave cheesecake and don't have time to make a whole cake, in just 20 minutes you can make these velvety, tangerine-infused bites.

1. Preheat oven to 350°F. Line an 8×8×2-inch baking pan with foil, extending the foil over edges of pan; set aside.

2. For crust, in a small mixing bowl beat butter and brown sugar with a mixer on medium to high until light and fluffy. Add flour, beating until combined (mixture will be crumbly). Press crust evenly into the prepared pan. Bake for 8 minutes.

3. Meanwhile, for filling, in a medium mixing bowl beat cream cheese and granulated sugar with a mixer on medium until smooth. Beat in egg, whipping cream, the finely shredded tangerine peel, tangerine juice, and vanilla until combined. Pour filling over crust.

4. Bake for 30 minutes more or just until filling is set. Cool in pan on a wire rack for 1 hour. Cover and chill for at least 2 hours. Lift uncut bars from pan. Cut into squares or triangles. If desired, sprinkle with candied tangerine peel.

FOR 32 SERVINGS In Step 1 use a 13×9×2-inch baking pan.

PER SERVING *166 cal., 12 g fat (7 g sat. fat), 48 mg chol., 101 mg sodium, 13 g carb., 0 g fiber, 2 g pro.*

PREP 20 minutes   BAKE 38 minutes at 350°F
COOL 1 hour   CHILL 2 hours

16 servings	ingredients	32 servings
¼ cup	butter, softened	½ cup
¼ cup	packed brown sugar	½ cup
⅔ cup	all-purpose flour	1⅓ cups
12 oz.	cream cheese, softened	three 8-oz. pkg.
⅓ cup	granulated sugar	⅔ cup
1	egg	2
¼ cup	whipping cream	½ cup
2 tsp.	finely shredded tangerine peel	4 tsp.
3 Tbsp.	tangerine juice	6 Tbsp.
½ tsp.	vanilla	1 tsp.
	Candied tangerine peel (optional)	

Raspberry-Maple Bars

Use either light or dark brown sugar in these fruited bars. Dark brown sugar intensifies the warm, caramelly flavor. Light brown sugar offers a subtle sweetness.

1. Preheat oven to 350°F. Line an 8×8×2-inch baking pan with foil, extending the foil over edges of pan. Grease foil; set pan aside.

2. In a medium saucepan stir brown sugar, the ⅓ cup butter, and the ¼ cup maple syrup over medium heat until butter is melted and mixture is smooth. Remove from heat; cool slightly. Stir in egg and vanilla. Stir in flour, baking powder, and baking soda until combined. Gently stir in raspberries.

3. Pour batter into the prepared baking pan, spreading evenly. Bake for 25 to 30 minutes or until a wooden toothpick inserted in the center comes out clean. Cool in pan on a wire rack.

4. For frosting, in a medium bowl stir together powdered sugar, the 2 tablespoons maple syrup, the 1 tablespoon softened butter, and the milk until smooth. Spread frosting on cooled bars. Spoon raspberry preserves in small mounds on frosting. Using a narrow metal spatula or a table knife, swirl slightly to marble. Using the edges of the foil, lift uncut bars from pan. Cut into bars.

FOR 36 SERVINGS In Step 1 use a 13×9×2-inch baking pan. In Step 2 use ⅔ cup butter and ½ cup maple syrup. In Step 4 use ¼ cup maple syrup and 2 tablespoons softened butter.

PER SERVING *147 cal., 4 g fat (3 g sat. fat), 21 mg chol., 66 mg sodium, 26 g carb., 0 g fiber, 1 g pro.*

PREP 30 minutes
BAKE 25 minutes at 350°F

18 servings	ingredients	36 servings
¾ cup	packed brown sugar	1¼ cups
⅓ cup	butter	⅔ cup
¼ cup	maple syrup	½ cup
1	egg	2
1 tsp.	vanilla	2 tsp.
1 cup	all-purpose flour	2 cups
½ tsp.	baking powder	1 tsp.
⅛ tsp.	baking soda	¼ tsp.
½ cup	frozen raspberries	1 cup
1 cup	powdered sugar	2 cups
2 Tbsp.	maple syrup	¼ cup
1 Tbsp.	butter, softened	2 Tbsp.
1 Tbsp.	milk	2 Tbsp.
2 Tbsp.	raspberry preserves	¼ cup

Carrot and Zucchini Bars

The colorful confetti of shredded carrots and zucchini makes these bars super moist.

PREP 20 minutes
BAKE 25 minutes at 350°F

18 servings	ingredients	36 servings
¾ cup	all-purpose flour	1½ cups
½ tsp.	baking powder	1 tsp.
¼ tsp.	ground ginger	½ tsp.
⅛ tsp.	baking soda	¼ tsp.
1	egg, lightly beaten	2
¾ cup	shredded carrots	1½ cups
½ cup	shredded zucchini	1 cup
⅓ cup	packed brown sugar	¾ cup
¼ cup	raisins	½ cup
¼ cup	chopped walnuts	½ cup
¼ cup	canola oil	½ cup
2 Tbsp.	honey	¼ cup
½ tsp.	vanilla	1 tsp.
half 8-oz. pkg.	cream cheese, softened	one 8-oz. pkg.
½ cup	powdered sugar	1 cup
½ tsp.	finely shredded lemon or orange peel	1 tsp.

1. Preheat oven to 350°F. In a large bowl stir together flour, baking powder, ginger, and baking soda; set aside.

2. In a medium bowl combine egg, carrots, zucchini, brown sugar, raisins, walnuts, oil, honey, and vanilla. Add carrot mixture to flour mixture, stirring just until combined. Spread batter in an ungreased 8×8×2-inch baking pan.

3. Bake for 25 minutes or until a wooden toothpick inserted in the center comes out clean. Cool in pan on a wire rack.

4. Meanwhile, for the citrus-cream-cheese frosting, in a medium bowl beat cream cheese and powdered sugar with a mixer on medium until fluffy. Stir in lemon peel. Frost uncut bars. Cut into bars.

FOR 36 SERVINGS In Step 2 use a 13×9×2-inch baking pan.

PER SERVING *125 cal., 7 g fat (2 g sat. fat), 19 mg chol., 44 mg sodium, 16 g carb., 1 g fiber, 2 g pro.*

Iced Walnut Shortbread Rounds

Cream cheese adds tenderness and subtle tanginess to these rich, buttery cookies.

14 servings	ingredients	28 servings
1¼ cups	all-purpose flour	2½ cups
½ cup	toasted walnuts, ground (see tip, page 24)	1 cup
¼ cup	granulated sugar	½ cup
⅛ tsp.	salt	¼ tsp.
½ cup	butter	1 cup
2 oz.	cream cheese, softened	4 oz.
2 Tbsp.	butter, softened	¼ cup
1 cup	powdered sugar	2 cups
	Milk	
	Coarse sugar or granulated sugar (optional)	

1. Preheat oven to 325°F. In a large bowl stir together flour, ground walnuts, the ¼ cup granulated sugar, and the salt. Using a pastry blender, cut in the ½ cup butter until mixture resembles fine crumbs and starts to cling. Form dough into a ball and knead until smooth.

2. On a lightly floured surface, roll dough to ¼-inch thickness. Using a 2-inch scalloped round cookie cutter, cut out dough. Place cutouts on a large ungreased cookie sheet.

3. Bake for 18 to 22 minutes or just until edges start to brown. Transfer cookies to a wire rack; cool.

4. For icing, in a medium mixing bowl beat cream cheese and the 2 tablespoons butter with a mixer on medium until smooth. Gradually add powdered sugar, beating until combined. Beat in enough milk for icing to reach drizzling consistency. Drizzle icing over cookies. If desired, sprinkle cookies with coarse sugar.

FOR 28 SERVINGS In Step 1 use ½ cup granulated sugar and 1 cup butter. In Step 4 use the ¼ cup softened butter.

PER SERVING *196 cal., 12 g fat (6 g sat. fat), 26 mg chol., 105 mg sodium, 22 g carb., 0 g fiber, 2 g pro.*

Salty-Sweet Butterscotch Cookies

If you like, sprinkle a tiny bit of flaked sea salt on the top of each scoop of cookie dough before baking the cookies.

1. Preheat oven to 375°F. In a large mixing bowl beat butter with a mixer on medium to high for 30 seconds. Add granulated sugar, brown sugar, baking powder, baking soda, and salt. Beat until combined, scraping sides of bowl occasionally. Beat in eggs and vanilla until combined. Beat in as much of the flour as you can with the mixer. Using a wooden spoon, stir in any remaining flour, the cashews, and butterscotch pieces.

2. Drop dough by rounded teaspoons 2 inches apart onto an ungreased cookie sheet. Bake for 8 to 10 minutes or until edges are lightly browned. Cool on cookie sheet for 2 minutes. Transfer cookies to a wire rack; cool.

PER SERVING *81 cal., 3 g fat (2 g sat. fat), 10 mg chol., 68 mg sodium, 12 g carb., 0 g fiber, 1 g pro.*

PREP 35 minutes
BAKE 8 minutes at 375°F   COOL 2 minutes

30 servings	ingredients	60 servings
¼ cup	butter, softened	½ cup
½ cup	granulated sugar	1 cup
½ cup	packed brown sugar	1 cup
½ tsp.	baking powder	1 tsp.
¼ tsp.	baking soda	½ tsp.
¼ tsp.	salt	½ tsp.
2	eggs	4
1 tsp.	vanilla	2 tsp.
1 cup	white whole wheat flour or all-purpose flour	2 cups
⅓ cup	coarsely chopped salted dry-roasted cashews	¾ cup
⅓ cup	butterscotch-flavor pieces	⅔ cup

Chocolate-Marshmallow Cookies

These whimsical treats taste a bit like a familiar chocolate-and-marshmallow cookie that can be found in the cookie aisle of almost any supermarket — only much better.

1. Preheat oven to 375°F. In a large mixing bowl beat butter and shortening with a mixer on medium to high for 30 seconds. Add granulated sugar, brown sugar, baking soda, and salt. Beat until combined, scraping sides of bowl occasionally. Beat in egg and vanilla until combined. Beat in cocoa powder. Beat in as much of the flour as you can with the mixer. Using a wooden spoon, stir in any remaining flour.

2. Drop dough by rounded teaspoons 2 inches apart onto an ungreased cookie sheet (or use a small to medium cookie scoop to drop dough). Spoon marshmallow creme into a pastry bag fitted with a small round (¼-inch) tip. Insert the tip into each mound of dough and squeeze a small amount of the marshmallow creme into each mound.

3. Bake for 8 to 9 minutes or until edges are firm. Cool on cookie sheet for 2 minutes. Transfer cookies to a wire rack; cool.

4. For icing, in a small saucepan stir chocolate pieces and sweetened condensed milk over low heat until melted and smooth. Stir in the milk. If necessary, stir in additional milk, ½ teaspoon at a time, to reach glazing consistency. Spread cookies with icing. Let stand until icing is set.

PER SERVING *137 cal., 6 g fat (3 g sat. fat), 14 mg chol., 80 mg sodium, 19 g carb., 1 g fiber, 2 g pro.*

PREP 35 minutes
BAKE 8 minutes at 375°F
COOL 2 minutes

24 servings	ingredients	48 servings
¼ cup	butter, softened	½ cup
¼ cup	shortening	½ cup
½ cup	granulated sugar	1 cup
¼ cup	packed brown sugar	½ cup
½ tsp.	baking soda	1 tsp.
¼ tsp.	salt	½ tsp.
1	egg	2
½ tsp.	vanilla	1 tsp.
2 Tbsp.	unsweetened cocoa powder	¼ cup
1¼ cups	all-purpose flour	2½ cups
⅓ cup	marshmallow creme	¾ cup
¾ cup	semisweet chocolate pieces	1½ cups
⅓ cup	sweetened condensed milk	¾ cup
½ Tbsp.	milk	1 Tbsp.
	Milk (optional)	

Brown Sugar S'more Drops

PREP 35 minutes
BAKE 8 minutes at 375°F
COOL 2 minutes

24 servings	ingredients	48 servings
¼ cup	butter, softened	½ cup
¼ cup	shortening	½ cup
½ cup	packed brown sugar	1 cup
¼ cup	granulated sugar	½ cup
¼ tsp.	baking soda	½ tsp.
¼ tsp.	salt	½ tsp.
1	egg	2
½ tsp.	vanilla	1 tsp.
1¼ cups	all-purpose flour	2½ cups
½ cup	tiny marshmallows	1 cup
½ cup	chopped milk chocolate	1 cup
¼ cup	crushed graham crackers	½ cup

Crushed graham crackers, chopped milk chocolate and itty-bitty marshmallows give these simple drop cookies the taste of those favorite fireside treats.

1. Preheat oven to 375°F. Line a cookie sheet with parchment paper; set aside. In a large mixing bowl beat butter and shortening with a mixer on medium to high for 30 seconds. Add brown sugar, granulated sugar, baking soda, and salt. Beat until combined, scraping sides of bowl occasionally. Beat in egg and vanilla until combined. Beat in as much of the flour as you can with the mixer. Using a wooden spoon, stir in any remaining flour, the marshmallows, chocolate, and crushed graham crackers.

2. Drop dough by rounded teaspoons 2 inches apart onto the prepared cookie sheet. Bake for 8 to 9 minutes or until lightly browned. Cool on cookie sheet for 2 minutes. Transfer cookies to a wire rack; cool.

PER SERVING *90 cal., 4 g fat (2 g sat. fat), 14 mg chol., 55 mg sodium, 12 g carb., 0 g fiber, 1 g pro.*

Creamy Cherry Dips

A dozen of these darling cookies packed in a pretty box makes a welcome gift for Valentine's, Mother's Day, or a birthday.

1. For filling, in a medium mixing bowl beat cream cheese and powdered sugar with a mixer on medium until smooth. Stir in cherries and almond extract. Spread filling on bottoms of half the vanilla wafers. Top with the remaining wafers, bottom sides down. Cover and chill about 30 minutes or until filling is firm.

2. Spread waxed paper on baking sheets. Seta side. In a medium saucepan stir chocolate candy coating and shortening over low heat until melted and smooth. Remove from heat. Using a fork, dip each sandwich cookie in melted chocolate coating, turning to coat completely and letting excess coating drip back into pan. Place dipped cookies on a sheet of waxed paper. Sprinkle with jimmies. Let stand for 30 minutes or until chocolate coating is set.

***TIP** If you prefer, use microwave oven to melt chocolate-flavor candy coating. In a small microwave-safe bowl combine candy coating and shortening. Microwave on high for 30 to 60 seconds or until coating is melted and mixture is smooth, stirring every 30 seconds.

PER SERVING 133 cal., 7 g fat (4 g sat. fat), 4 mg chol., 56 mg sodium, 17 g carb., 0 g fiber, 1 g pro.

PREP 30 minutes
CHILL 30 minutes
STAND 30 minutes

30 servings	ingredients	60 servings
half 8-oz. pkg.	cream cheese, softened	one 8-oz. pkg.
½ cup	powdered sugar	1 cup
½ cup	finely chopped, drained maraschino cherries	1 cup
¼ tsp.	almond extract	½ tsp.
60	vanilla wafers	120
12 oz.	chocolate-flavor candy coating, coarsely chopped	24 oz.
2 tsp.	shortening	4 tsp.
	Jimmies or decors	

Index

Metric Information

PRODUCT DIFFERENCES

Most of the ingredients called for in the recipes in this book are available in most countries. However, some are known by different names. Here are some common American ingredients and their possible counterparts:

- Sugar (white) is granulated, fine granulated, or castor sugar.
- Powdered sugar is icing sugar.
- All-purpose flour is enriched bleached, or unbleached white household flour. When self-rising flour is used in place of all-purpose flour in a recipe that calls for leavening, omit the leavening agent (baking soda or baking powder) and salt.
- Light-color corn syrup is golden syrup.
- Cornstarch is cornflour.
- Baking soda is bicarbonate of soda.
- Vanilla or vanilla extract is vanilla essence.
- Green, red, or yellow sweet peppers are capsicums or bell peppers.
- Golden raisins are sultanas.

VOLUME AND WEIGHT

The United States traditionally uses cup measures for liquid and solid ingredients. The chart (above right) shows the approximate imperial and metric equivalents. If you are accustomed to weighing solid ingredients, the following approximate equivalents will be helpful.

- 1 cup butter, castor sugar, or rice = 8 ounces = ½ pound = 250 grams
- 1 cup flour = 4 ounces = ¼ pound = 125 grams
- 1 cup icing sugar = 5 ounces = 150 grams
- Canadian and U.S. volume for a cup measure is 8 fluid ounces (237 ml), but the standard metric equivalent is 250 ml.
- 1 British imperial cup is 10 fluid ounces.
- In Australia, 1 tablespoon equals 20 ml, and there are 4 teaspoons in the Australian tablespoon.
- Spoon measures are used for small amounts of ingredients. Although the size of the tablespoon varies slightly in different countries, for practical purposes and for recipes in this book, a straight substitution is all that's necessary. Measurements made using cups or spoons always should be level unless stated otherwise.

COMMON WEIGHT RANGE REPLACEMENTS

Imperial / U.S.	Metric
½ ounce	15 g
1 ounce	25 g or 30 g
4 ounces (¼ pound)	115 g or 125 g
8 ounces (½ pound)	225 g or 250 g
16 ounces (1 pound)	450 g or 500 g
1¼ pounds	625 g
1½ pounds	750 g
2 pounds or 2¼ pounds	1,000 g or 1 Kg

OVEN TEMPERATURE EQUIVALENTS

Fahrenheit Setting	Celsius Setting	Gas Setting
300°F	150°C	Gas Mark 2 (very low)
325°F	160°C	Gas Mark 3 (low)
350°F	180°C	Gas Mark 4 (moderate)
375°F	190°C	Gas Mark 5 (moderate)
400°F	200°C	Gas Mark 6 (hot)
425°F	220°C	Gas Mark 7 (hot)
450°F	230°C	Gas Mark 8 (very hot)
475°F	240°C	Gas Mark 9 (very hot)
500°F	260°C	Gas Mark 10 (extremely hot)
Broil	Broil	Grill

*Electric and gas ovens may be calibrated using celsius. However, for an electric oven, increase celsius setting 10 to 20 degrees when cooking above 160°C. For convection or forced air ovens (gas or electric), lower the temperature setting 25°F/10°C when cooking at all heat levels.

BAKING PAN SIZES

Imperial / U.S.	Metric
9×1½-inch round cake pan	22- or 23×4-cm (1.5 L)
9×1½-inch pie plate	22- or 23×4-cm (1 L)
8×8×2-inch square cake pan	20×5-cm (2 L)
9×9×2-inch square cake pan	22- or 23×4.5-cm (2.5 L)
11×7×1½-inch baking pan	28×17×4-cm (2 L)
2-quart rectangular baking pan	30×19×4.5-cm (3 L)
13×9×2-inch baking pan	34×22×4.5-cm (3.5 L)
15×10×1-inch jelly roll pan	40×25×2-cm
9×5×3-inch loaf pan	23×13×8-cm (2 L)
2-quart casserole	2 L

U.S./STANDARD METRIC EQUIVALENTS

⅛ teaspoon = 0.5 ml	
¼ teaspoon = 1 ml	
½ teaspoon = 2 ml	
1 teaspoon = 5 ml	
1 tablespoon = 15 ml	
2 tablespoons = 25 ml	
¼ cup = 2 fluid ounces = 50 ml	
⅓ cup = 3 fluid ounces = 75 ml	
½ cup = 4 fluid ounces = 125 ml	
⅔ cup = 5 fluid ounces = 150 ml	
¾ cup = 6 fluid ounces = 175 ml	
1 cup = 8 fluid ounces = 250 ml	
2 cups = 1 pint = 500 ml	
1 quart = 1 litre	